The Conflict Pivot

Also by Tammy Lenski

Making Mediation Your Day Job

Out beyond ideas of wrong-doing and right-doing,
there is a field. I will meet you there.
—Rumi

For Pepi and Rod,
beloved buoys

CONTENTS

INTRODUCTION

Jen, a mediation graduate student in my Interpersonal Conflict course, pointed to an excellent conflict resolution book we'd just read and said, "I love this book. And I hate it, too. It's got so much to teach me, but I won't remember it all. I just can't keep track of that much advice."

She'd just summarized my own experience with favorite conflict resolution books and a protest I'd heard before: the sense that the best conflict resolution books help us understand our conflicts in fresh ways, yet can overwhelm us in the process. We love what we're reading, yet can't retain enough of it for use later.

A few years afterward, in a later version of the same course, another graduate student put out his hands in a supplicating gesture. Kregg said, "When I'm frustrated I need something really simple to latch onto, not a long recipe of possibilities to try. I can probably handle remembering three things when I'm stressed. Why can't anyone show me how to do that?"

He was right. In the heat of the moment, most of us don't have the wherewithal to sort through a series of mental recipe cards, looking for and then selecting the approach that will help us then and there. Kregg and Jen, two very smart graduate students, couldn't do it. I can't do it consistently either—and I am a professional conflict resolver.

Jen's and Kregg's comments left me pondering, *What three things can make the most difference in the way a conflict unfolds?*

Business partners Chris and Avery[1] asked me to help them sort out a difference of opinion about how to run the small eight-person company they had cofounded. Things had gotten bad enough that neither partner was talking to the other, communicating only via their shared executive assistant (poor woman). When the mediation was over and they'd come to agreement over the issues that had divided them for many months, we sat together over coffee and mused about the trajectory their conflict had taken over the past year. Chris said, "With the benefit of hindsight, I see now that either of us could have prevented the problem from escalating. I could have stopped the momentum by doing one or two things differently anywhere along the way. But I felt powerless to change what was happening without Avery also joining the effort." Avery nodded, agreeing with the sentiment.

We find ourselves in conflict with others who share our work and our lives—people with whom we want or need to be in continuing relationships—and we figure that since it took two (or more) of us to create the conflict, it's going to take two (or more) of us to resolve it. But is that necessarily true? It's not.

Chris's comment left me musing, *How can we*

*dramatically shift a conflict without relying on what the other person
will or won't do?*

Nicole, a telecommunications executive who deals
with complex problems all day long, wanted to find a
better response to long-term conflicts with her spouse.
There were problems the two of them just couldn't seem
to put to rest. It was maddening to Nicole that she was so
admired as a fixer at work, yet she couldn't achieve the
same results at home. As we explored what would help
provide some relief for their relationship, she said, "I
think my goals have been wrong. Resolution or 'fixing'
aren't what really matter. What I care about most is
dissolving the tension and keeping the problem from
getting in our way. I want to prevent conflict from
eroding our joy and love."

Her comment was spot on. When in conflict with
those we're closest to, it's tempting to focus on the
presenting problem of the moment: Should the person
who empties the coffeepot be responsible for making
fresh coffee? Was that project deadline reasonable?
Whose turn is it to fold the laundry? Answering those
questions may yield momentary relief, yes. But if we're in
an ongoing state of tension with someone, those answers
will be Band-Aids at best. Another presenting problem
will be waiting for us tomorrow, wearing us down while
at the same time building up the wall between us.

Nicole's clarity left me to figure out, *What can help us
move beyond a state of chronic conflict in our most important
relationships at work and home?*

These three questions resonated deeply. I've been in
the conflict resolution field for a while now, and I'd like
to think I know a useful thing or two. I've mediated
thousands of disputes in person and online, coached
hundreds in successfully navigating conflict, taught

negotiation and conflict resolution in several graduate programs, and trained hundreds of new and seasoned mediators in mastering our craft. In all of this work, I could see clients and students challenged over and over again in the same ways that Jen, Kregg, Chris, Avery, and Nicole were.

And I could not help but notice that some of my own conflicts would benefit immensely from answers to the same three questions. When I tried to take what I know as a professional conflict resolver and use it in my own life, the results were mixed. Sometimes I handled things quite well. Sometimes I prayed no one who knows what I do for a living was watching at that moment because if they were, I'd be obligated to have "fraud" tattooed on my forehead.

When I tried to remember long conflict resolution recipes during high-heat moments, too often the result was my own muddled mind. Approaches that work well with concrete disputes, like those involving a policy change or the amount of money to spend on new kitchen cabinets, worked dismally in states of tension and conflict. And I intensely disliked the helplessness I felt when I couldn't persuade someone else to join me in collaborating on a cessation of hostilities, and so the conflict remained, hovering in the air between us.

Jen, Kregg, Chris, Avery, and Nicole launched me on a quest to identify a simple, straightforward approach that addressed the questions born from their comments. I wanted an approach that is memorable, with a visual metaphor—an idea that ultimately led to "pivots"—to help anchor the concept in your mind for easier retrieval when you need it most. I wanted an approach that would help people avoid the most common conflict pitfalls I witness repeatedly while working with clients. I wanted the approach to be easily learnable and one that would be useful with any kind of conflict in an ongoing personal, professional, or business relationship, the very conflicts that fray us at the edges if we don't address them. And I wanted an approach that could head off the escalation of some of life's simpler conflicts and help you get your feet back under you before you're off to the races. It was a tall order.

For the last decade I have been experimenting on myself (and my exceedingly patient husband), putting ideas to the test with clients, getting feedback from my graduate students, then refining and reworking, distilling and paring. The quest has brought us to this book and to the three conflict pivots described in the coming pages.[2]

The Conflict Pivot is organized to give you immediate access to the approach so that you can begin experimenting with it today, if you wish. Part 1 of the book introduces the pivot practices. Chapter 1 describes the guiding principles on which the three conflict pivots are based and why they matter. And lest you mistakenly believe the pivots can fix all conflict that ails you, I discuss the value that conflict has in our lives and ways to use the pivots not just to get past conflict, but to develop a healthier relationship with it. In chapter 2, I briefly introduce the three pivots and provide a worksheet you can use to walk yourself through the three practices.

Part 2 focuses on each of the pivots in detail and is intended to build your fluency with them. Chapters 3, 4, and 5 take a deeper dive into each pivot, offering you depth of understanding for better mastery. I share examples from my own life and from situations clients have faced. Seeing how others have handled conflict pivots can offer insight into your own.

Part 3 wraps up the book. In chapter 6, I address the

questions clients and workshop participants have asked most frequently about the pivots, hoping that in so doing I'm answering remaining questions on your mind as well. In chapter 7, I discuss ways to begin applying the pivots in your life and work. I suggest ways to practice pivoting so that it becomes a habit, a reflex action during conflict that can, over time, overtake the less beneficial habits you may have now. Together, these latter chapters are there to help you assimilate the pivots into daily life.

The conflict pivots best shine a light into the darkness when you make them your own.

PART 1
THE BASICS

1

ON PIVOTING

In business, a pivot is a strategic change in a company's direction, motivated by opportunity for greater success. In basketball, a pivot is a rotation to face another direction in order to pass or shoot the ball more effectively. In conflict, a pivot follows the same idea: change the direction you're focusing in order to achieve better results.

You can make a state of conflict better, even one that's bedeviled you for years. You can resolve conflict before it festers and begins to gnaw at the edges of your soul, even if the thought of confrontation makes you break out in a cold sweat. You can stop a minor skirmish in its tracks before it sucks you in. You can change how you react in conflict situations, whether you're a conflict coward, a conflict junkie, or somewhere in between. And you can transform a conflict into peace of mind relying solely on your own thoughts and actions.

This is a book about having less conflict in your life, strengthening the business and personal relationships that matter most, and making conflict resolution simpler. It teaches you a way to think about conflict so you can unlock it, address it, and move on with your life. Epictetus said, "People are disturbed not by things, but by the view they take of them." Each conflict pivot is a concise thought process, a mental exercise intended to coax your mind into dealing with your conflict in a new way, experiencing it as an interested observer instead of an aggrieved sufferer.

You can use the pivot practices on your own, anytime, anyplace, without relying on what the other person will or won't do. With the three conflict pivots, you will be able to achieve one of two things with any conflict on an ongoing personal or professional relationship:

1. Truly let it go and move on. Annie Proulx said, "If you can't fix it you've got to stand it." One way to stand it is to figure out how to let it go.
2. Know precisely what you should discuss with the other person so that real resolution between you is within your grasp.

Use the pivot practices regularly and you'll find that some of the things that eat at you are things you can learn to let go. There are conflicts that, though they may once have loomed large, turn out not to matter in your life. Life is short, and knowing how to let go and move on is a good thing. It's certainly a good thing for me to have learned. I like to joke that before I taught myself how to let go and move on, I seemed to be about five feet tall. With all that extra figurative weight off my shoulders, it turns out that I'm considerably taller.

Use the practices regularly and you'll know how to tell the ones you should let go from the ones you shouldn't.

Occasionally, a conflict is one of the truly important ones in your life and involves someone with whom you have a close personal or professional relationship. In those instances, trying to let it go probably won't succeed and will be a mistake that'll still haunt you years from now.

For the ones that really do matter, the practices this book teaches will help you focus on the right problem when you talk it out. Most people don't focus on the right problem when they confront a conflict. It makes for a big waste of time, a lot of frustration, and, occasionally, histrionics we'd all be happier not to witness.

Use the practices regularly and they'll help you avoid some of the most common mistakes people make while in conflict. We make these mistakes because we're imperfect beings and mistake making is part of the human condition. Conflict causes our best selves to flee into the closet and hide behind the heavy winter coats, so most of us are even less capable of avoiding mistakes when the air is thick with tension. I've been known to fall into those traps myself, even though I'm a mediator and know better. How wealthy I would be now if I had long ago thought to charge my clients neither by the hour nor the value of my work, but by the frequency with which I witness people falling into these traps:

- equating your version of what happened with The Truth
- blaming the other person for the discomfort you're experiencing in the conflict
- spending far too much time on what happened in the past and too little on what you will do from here forward

Use the practices regularly and you'll learn how to replace habits doomed to get you stuck with habits that truly set you free. In her poem *Autobiography in Five Short Chapters*[1] Portia Nelson muses about the figurative experience of repeatedly walking down a certain street and falling in the same deep hole in the sidewalk. Each stanza of the poem begins with a similar sequence: "I walk down the street. There is a deep hole in the sidewalk. I fall in." At first, as she struggles to get out of the hole, she is sure it isn't her fault that she fell in. After several instances, she begins to see that her choices are indeed the cause of her repeated plunges into the hole in the sidewalk and this awareness helps her climb out more successfully. Eventually she learns to watch for the deep hole as she walks down the sidewalk and to walk around it.

That's where most of us stop in conflict with someone close to us, too: we watch for it and try to navigate around it. That's not a terrible approach, but it leaves us forever cautious and vigilant and isn't the stuff of vibrant, relaxed personal and professional relationships.

The final stanza of Nelson's poem is a single line that shows us how refreshing it can be to truly change a habit. When I read the poem out loud to others, invariably the listener laughs in delight. The last stanza of the poem is this: "I walk down another street."

The conflict pivot practices are intended to help you walk around the deep holes in your sidewalk and, once they become habit, to help you walk down another street.

The following guiding principles give form and shape to the pivots. Collectively they serve as a road map for finding a new street to walk down during conflict.

Our Story of the Conflict
Is Not *the* Story of the Conflict

We dwell on certain parts of any conflict, replaying those parts in our minds and in the stories we tell others about the conflict. In ongoing conflict we dwell so much on these parts that they begin to feel like The Truth. To make matters worse, our conflict stories tend to focus too much attention on the other person's behavior, their (bad) intentions, and their flaws. Sometimes our stories also cause us to dwell on our own frailties and our shadow selves, causing far too much self-flagellation.

I call these Stuck Stories. Like a personal movie trailer, your stuck story of the conflict is a montage of the moments most interesting to you, with certain scenes magnified and others omitted. It's not *the* story of the conflict; it's *your* story of the conflict. The moments you recall and retell tend to be the ones that ticked you off the most, hurt you the most, or left you most troubled. They're the ones you use to justify your response. They're also the ones that have an important message for you, if you know how to listen for it. Now is the time to "tune your ears" to the signal your story is trying to give you.

Let's rewrite the story of our conflicts.

The Source of Our Discomfort Is Us,
Not Them

A friend was sitting at her desk one day, her beloved yellow lab at her feet. Suddenly, the dog jumped, yelped, and turned to look up at her. She looked down at the dog, wondering what had happened. This scene repeated itself several more times, and the dog's gaze at her became increasingly accusatory. Finally, he got up and left the room.

It turned out that the dog had a pinched nerve in his back. She asked the vet why the dog had repeatedly looked up at her each time he felt the pain. Was he begging her for help? No, speculated the vet, he was looking for the source of the pain and you were the only thing close enough to be hurting him.

Dogs aren't the only ones who reach conclusions like this. When you are in conflict with someone, you may look outward for the source of your discomfort and pinpoint the other person's words or actions as the cause. There they are, right in front of you, after all.

You would do better to look within. You are feeling discomfort for an important reason and when you discern that reason, you will have an important key for unlocking the conflict.

Let's figure out what our discomfort is really telling us.

Relief Comes from the Now, Not from the Past

Two monks, Tanzan and Ekido, were walking together down a muddy road. A heavy rain was falling and had swollen the stream running near the path. Rounding a bend, they saw a beautiful girl dressed in formal kimono, crying at the edge of the stream.

Tanzan asked, "What is wrong?" The girl explained that she was on her way to a wedding and could not cross the muddy stream without ruining her kimono. "Come," said Tanzan, reaching out his arms. Lifting her, he carried her across the muddy stream and set her down on the other side. Then, the monks continued on their way.

Ekido did not speak until they reached their destination, the temple. Then, angrily, he said to Tanzan, "You know that monks do not touch females. You should not have done that!"

"I left the girl back on the path," replied Tanzan. "Why are you still carrying her?"[2]

For most of us, conflict is a trap of the past. We spend time thinking and talking about who did what, who said what, what they or we should have done differently, who was wrong, and who was right. Some of us are so committed to dwelling on what happened that it becomes a strange kind of torturous self-soothing to think about it over and over. We keep carrying it, like the monk Ekido—into the shower, on our morning run, in phone conversations with our best friend, in sleepless moments at 2:00 a.m.

When I mentor new mediators, one of the questions they most frequently ask me is, "How do I get them off the gerbil-wheel of the past?" They see their clients lured into rehashing the past, unable to stop themselves, so hooked by what happened that they cannot get free, going around and around like a gerbil running on its little wheel.

While conflict can be a trap of the past, conflict resolution is an act of the present and the future. You cannot resolve conflict unless you can figure out a way to face forward. Understanding the past will only get you so far, and if you're looking backward with each forward step you take, you already know the inevitable tumble that's coming. Better to pivot, turn your back on what can't be changed, and turn toward what can.

Let's face forward.

Complicated Stuff Doesn't Need
More Complication—It Needs Less

In *Say NO by Default,* author Derek Sivers tells a story about Steve Jobs privately presenting the then-new iTunes Music Store to an independent record label group. People in the room kept asking whether iTunes had certain features and when certain other features would be added. Jobs finally said, "Wait, wait—put your hands down. Listen: I know you have a thousand ideas for all the cool features iTunes could have. So do we. But we don't want a thousand features. That would be ugly. Innovation is not about saying yes to everything. It's about saying no to all but the most crucial features."[3]

Like software that gets larger and more complex with each version, many approaches to conflict resolution suffer from feature creep and bloat. Those of us working and writing in the conflict resolution field see conflict in such richness, humans in such complexity, and problem solving as a tapestry woven of a thousand threads. We mistakenly conflate the complexity we observe in conflicts with what's needed to resolve them, and then we pass along that complexity to you.

Venture capitalist Guy Kawasaki has said that people need a guidepost,[4] an outline to help them wake up each day knowing why they want to go to work. I think people in conflict need guideposts too, something to rely on so we know with each difficult conversation why we're there and what we can do about it.

Most of us already know how to make our conflicts complex. Let's stop and do something different. Jobs said, "You have to work hard to get your thinking clean to make it simple. But it's worth it in the end because once you get there, you can move mountains."[5]

Let's clean up and simplify our thinking about our conflicts—and move mountains.

Release from Conflict Can Be a Solo Act

Conflict resolution is generally understood as a joint exercise, something that involves the person or persons we're in conflict with. When we hear the term *conflict resolution* we're likely to imagine it as some kind of conversation or negotiation with another person. That would not be inaccurate.

But it would be incomplete. What happens when the negotiation you most need to have is with yourself? What happens when the thing you most need to understand, address, and move on from is something only you yourself have the key to unlock? I've noticed that many conflicts, small and large, do not require conversation with another person to address properly. For many of the conflicts in your life, the conversation you most need to have is with yourself.

It is a good thing to be able to problem-solve collaboratively, and there are many good books on the subject, even some that help you navigate a conflict jointly despite the other person being a reticent negotiation partner. You should read those books. If you do what they tell you, they'll help you have a better life and probably have a positive effect on your career advancement.[6]

But sometimes, you can do those things and joint resolution of the conflict remains elusive. Conflict is a slippery sucker, replete with the complexities of human emotion, psyche, and behavior, ever unpredictable.

Superb negotiation cannot resolve all conflicts you experience with others in your life. You need, in those moments, to rely on yourself to find your way out.

When you make it the other person's job to resolve a conflict because, damn it, they started it (or it's their fault, they blew it, they did something bad to you, they don't take enough responsibility, they're selfish or mean, and so on), you hand a lot of your power to them. If you want to change the conflict, you must take your power back and change what *you* think about and do, because you're the only one you can count on to deliver. It is possible, sometimes even preferable, to resolve a conflict on your own. It can happen in shorter order than you might think and need not be an act of self-flagellation, long-term suffering, or endless belly button examination.

A friend, reading an early draft of this book, relayed a wonderful remark made to her years ago by a fellow she was dating. He said, "It doesn't take two to make a relationship—it really takes one."

Let's take power back. Let's be the one it takes.

Freedom Can Be More Important Than Joint Resolution

When I'm in the hot middle of my own conflict, I'm not particularly interested in managing it. In the midst of turbulence, "conflict management" feels almost ludicrous, like trying to contain a cat that's just fallen in a full bathtub.

I may want to resolve it, but "conflict resolution" has a sense about it, like a box wrapped in tissue paper and tied up with a pretty bow, that conveys the problem is fully sorted out, and nothing left amiss. In relationship conflict, that's an elusive goal. I fear that perpetually trying to reach that elusive goal leaves a lot of people suffering.

I would like to navigate the conflict better, yes. I'd like to engage it in a way that leaves me feeling good about the way I'm behaving, though I can say with absolute certainty that I will always aspire to this and with some frequency miss the mark. Neither "navigation" nor "engagement" fully speaks to me; neither echoes what I want in my soul.

What I really want when I'm in conflict with my husband is to be free from it. Not freedom as in avoidance, but freedom as in done well and moving on with our life together. What I really want when I'm in conflict with a fellow board member or a colleague is to finish it, minimize or eliminate damage to the relationship, and not let it eat too much of my tomorrow. I want freedom and peace of mind. I taught myself how to pivot in conflict so that I could have my freedom and peace of mind, and I offer them to you in that spirit.

Let's free ourselves.

On Changing Direction

Conflict pivots invite you to change the direction you're focusing in order to achieve a better outcome. This is not the same as ignoring everything that came before.

Changing direction helps you change your focus, but it doesn't erase everything else around you. Pivots don't mean that you must forget the past and ignore what has happened. Silicon Valley entrepreneur Eric Ries, credited with popularizing pivots as part of successful entrepreneurs' business strategy, said that successful startups change directions but stay grounded in what they've learned. "They keep one foot in the past and place one foot in a new possible future."[7] Similarly, a conflict pivot doesn't require you to dismiss the past as though it did not happen, but instead invites you to place your attention where you can still influence what happens: the present and the future.

The toughest part of freeing yourself from a conflict may be breaking away from the habits that have kept the conflict stuck. Those old habits are like well-worn clothing, comfortable and familiar, even if threadbare or ill fitting. In the novel *The Tragedy of Arthur*, the narrator captures an experience you may know all too well: "The next morning, on my way out of the apartment to the airport, my wife and I had one of those fights that are entirely unnecessary, in which everyone is simply reciting lines scripted by their worst impulses, a dull sequel to old fights, a dull prologue to later fights, a DVD frozen on the same stupid mid-blink face of a normally good-looking actor."

You know that dull prologue, those well-worn lines of script, ready and available whenever the next round of bickering begins. You also know that they can be difficult to banish, because they are almost rote now, habits as well ingrained as your morning cup of coffee, your cigarette, your reflexive reach for your cell phone to check e-mail while in the middle of a meeting. It will take commitment, but you can change the conflict habits that keep you stuck. Begin by setting aside your certainty and by emptying your cup, as this Zen koan, or traditional story, reminds us:

A university professor visited Nan-in to inquire about Zen. Nan-in served tea, pouring his visitor's cup full, and then continuing to pour. As the tea overflowed the cup and washed down the sides onto the table, the professor cried out, "Stop! It is full. No more will go in!"

"Like this cup," Nan-in said, "you are full of your own speculations and conclusions. How can I show you Zen unless you first empty your cup?"[8]

Not a Cure

It is no coincidence that I am writing a book on a subject that I have wrestled with personally. I come to you as a flawed human who tries daily to find better ways resolve conflict in my life. I bicker with my husband. Now and then I have a major clash with him. I find my friends occasionally irritating, and sometimes I respond in ways that others could legitimately call prickly or peevish. I have strong opinions on a few things that matter deeply to me and don't always handle myself well in contretemps about them. I lie awake at night when others judge me harshly for failing to handle a conflict well, even while noting the hypocrisy of being judged by others equally flawed.

I offer the pivots not because I want you to be healed, not because I think my job is to heal you, not because I think I have The Path you should follow, and not because I think your conflict needs to be fixed. Rather, I share the pivots as an offering from one strong and frail human to the next. I have found them freeing, and many of my clients have said the same. I hope they will be freeing to you as well.

But I don't hope freedom will come at the cost of deeper self-awareness. In the fall of 2013 I had the good fortune to spend several days at a scholarly retreat with Anglican diplomatic envoy and hostage negotiator Terry

Waite, himself held hostage and in almost total isolation for nearly five years by a Jihadist group during the late 1980s. One of the many wise things Waite said at the retreat was this: "We need to develop the ability to live creatively with conflict rather than allow conflict to deal negatively with us."

The pivots are not intended as an easy explanation for what ails you, followed by an efficient cure. Those are misbegotten goals; don't be lured by them. Rather, the pivots are intended as ways to orient your resources away from the things that keep you stuck and toward the things that can help get you unstuck. They are intended as one way to live more creatively with conflict.

Writer Thomas Moore has said that to be alive entails both the yin and yang of peace and pain. I want to ease suffering without easing it so much that you skitter over the surface of it, short-circuiting the meaning that suffering can hold out to you. I want to simplify the quagmire of conflict without tipping you into the realm of the simplistic. I want to help you toward new conclusions or understanding without letting the drive for resolution rush you past pain points that are rich with food for deeper thought. In Moore's words, "You have to sit with these things and in due time let them be revealed for what they are."[9]

2

THE WORKSHEET

We will examine each pivot in depth in part 2. Now, though, I want to give you a sense of the pivots and what they're asking of you. This chapter is intended to stand on its own as an independent worksheet anytime you need it.

To get the most from the rest of this book, take the time now to fill out the Conflict Pivot Worksheet for a conflict you're currently navigating or one that continues to haunt you even if it is no longer "active."

I recommend writing out your responses instead of working through the questions only in your head. Writing your responses forces you to say "out loud" thoughts that may be influencing your conflict. Writing them out gives you responses to refer back to later, as you move further down the worksheet and read further into the book, something many have told me is helpful. And writing them out allows the evolution of your thinking to be visible to you, a practice that can help you in future conflicts and until the pivoting practice becomes second nature. Moreover, a mounting body of research confirms that when you write about emotional experiences, significant physical and mental health improvements follow, including significant reductions in stress.[1]

A fill-in-the-blank worksheet is available for download. The Resources section at the end of the book provides you with web address and related information.

Pivot 1: Away from Your Stuck Story and Toward Its Message

The first conflict pivot is to stop ruminating on your stuck story and attend instead to what your stuck story is trying to tell you.

When you experience ongoing tension or conflict, you mentally replay what's happened as you attempt to understand it and figure out what to do. Over time, these replays lead to a shorthand story of the conflict that becomes polished in memory.

Like a movie trailer, your stuck story of the conflict is a montage of the most powerful and noteworthy moments, with certain scenes selected and others omitted. It's not *the* story of the conflict; it is *your* story of the conflict.

Your stuck story is rich with meaning if you know what to look for. Let's look now.

1. Who is the tension or conflict with and what is it about?

Example: *I have ongoing conflict with my husband, Jim, about the way he leaves me out of major financial and home decisions.*

2. To what have you reacted most strongly in the conflict?

Example: *In the conflict, I have reacted most strongly to hearing that Jim was meeting with realtors, and he hadn't even told me he wanted to buy a new house! I've also reacted strongly to finding out he has his own checking account separate from our joint checking account.*

Note: This question is not about what interpretation you reacted to strongly, but what thing(s) that <u>happened</u> most caused a reaction in you.

3. When you tell your story of the conflict to others or yourself, what do you focus on most?

Example: *When I tell my story of the conflict to others or myself, I dwell on the way Jim repeatedly makes important purchasing and financial decisions without me, how little regard he must have for my intelligence, and how much he likes to have power over me.*

Pivot 2: Away from Their Behavior and Toward Your Hooks

The second conflict pivot is to stop dwelling on the things the other person is doing or not doing and attend instead to the reasons you're hooked by the conflict.

States of conflict occur when something important feels threatened or insulted. The things you dwell on are hints about the true source of your unease in the conflict. You must attend to them to free yourself.

The list below, adapted from work by Dr. Stella Ting-Toomey, describes some of the most common "conflict hooks," those underlying reasons a conflict has snagged you. Conflict hooks are connected to your identity, the way you see yourself and want others to see you. When someone appears to challenge or dismiss what you hold dear about yourself, you get hooked (snagged by your discomfort).

While you may be hooked by any of the sources below, most of us tend to have one or two that are particularly strong and the most common source of frustration, tension, and conflict for us:

1. **Competence:** our need to be recognized as capable, intelligent, skilled, or having expertise
2. **Autonomy:** our need to be acknowledged as independent and self-reliant, and having our boundaries respected
3. **Fellowship:** our need to be included and to be viewed as likable, cooperative, and worthy
4. **Status:** our need to be admired for tangible and intangible assets such as attractiveness, reputation, power, and material worth
5. **Reliability:** our need to be seen as trustworthy, dependable, and loyal
6. **Integrity:** our need for others to respect our dignity, honor, virtue, and good character

While it is not absolutely necessary that the insult or threat you experience fall neatly into one of the above categories in order to have success with your conflict pivot, most people find that when they reflect deeply enough, one or more of the above applies.

4. Why do the things you listed in questions 2 and 3 bother you?

Example: *I'm bothered because I don't like being left out like a second-class citizen, I don't think a husband should have financial power over a wife, and I want to be seen as the smart person I am.*

5. What are the ways you see yourself that you suspect the other person may not?

Example: *I worry that Jim doesn't view me as smart, capable of contributing to good financial decisions, or as his intellectual equal.*

6. What conflict hooks have snagged you in this conflict?

Example: *I have been hooked by Jim's apparent disregard for my competence, my desire to be included in decisions (fellowship hook), and maybe also by my wish that he see me as his equal (status hook).*

Pivot 3: Away from the Past and Toward the Now

The third conflict pivot is to stop focusing on the past and attend instead to where your freedom lies—in what you do now.

Conflict thrives in the unknowable past—who said or did what, who's to blame, what really happened. Memory is very unreliable, even in instances where you feel quite certain you remember with great accuracy. Conflict resolution and choosing your freedom from a conflict are present- and future-focused acts.

Conflict also thrives in your reliance on the other person to set things right. When you rely on the other person to change what he or she is doing, and connect that person's actions to your happiness, you hand over power. The third pivot is about taking back your power, and rewriting your story of the conflict.

7. What are you protecting yourself *from*?

Example: *I am protecting myself from my fear that Jim views me as "the little woman," that I've married a man who does not see me as his equal. I'm protecting myself from the discomfort of admitting that I'm not as smart about finances as I pretend to be.*

8. What do you want for yourself from here forward in this situation?

Example: *I want to feel responsible and capable financially. I don't want to wonder all the time what he really thinks of me. I want there not to be constant tension and bickering about money. I want to be in a real partnership with my husband.*

9. What will you do to make this possible for yourself? List only those things that do not require the other person's actions or thinking to change.

Example: *I will take a personal financial management class and tell Jim I'm doing so. I will talk to Jim to find out whether it's even possible for him to view me as his equal and what it would take. I will not squabble constantly about the ways he leaves me out and will instead ask to be part of some decisions and build from there. I will use all of these experiences to determine whether or not this is the right marriage for me to remain in.*

PART 2
THE PIVOTS

3

THE FIRST PIVOT

Pivot Away from Your Stuck Story and Toward Its Message

"Maybe he's got a body in there," mused my husband.

I watched the man walking toward us, dragging something heavy behind him. Even from a long distance, it was easy to see that the load was a burden. "Maybe so," I said.

We were walking our dogs on one of the local rail trails on a cold winter day. As the distance between the man and us gr11ew smaller, we began to make up a story about the body inside what now appeared to be a large rolling suitcase. Perfect for body moving, we agreed, warming to our task.

As the man grew closer, we could see he was elderly and that the rolling suitcase was almost too heavy for him to pull behind him on this paved portion of the trail. "He may need our help," I said. My husband nodded, considering. Then he grinned and said, "But then wouldn't we be complicit in his crime?" We chuckled and went on with our story making.

We do this in conflict too: we make up stories. We make guesses to fill in blanks about things we don't understand in the situation or the other person. We take prior conclusions about the other person and use those conclusions to feed our guesses and judgments, forgetting that conclusions are just opinion, not fact. If we already have a poor history with the person, our stories tend to be tinged with darker tones. We tell these stories to ourselves and to others. This is not a malicious act; it is human to infer things as a way to figure out our world.

As the man approached us, we looked to make eye contact. He said hello tersely, then directed his gaze away from us and continued on. It was clear he didn't want to engage us.

As he passed, I glanced down at the heavy, bulging suitcase. Strapped to it with bungee cords was a chainsaw.

My head swiveled back toward my husband faster than Linda Blair's head spun around in *The Exorcist*. His eyes were as wide as mine. "Did you see that?" I squeaked. "He has a chainsaw!"

We started to giggle a little nervously, and then we roared at the shock of seeing the chainsaw after making up the dead body story. We'd reached the part of the trail where we usually turn around, so we began to head back with the dogs.

As we passed the section of the path where we'd been deep in conversation about the chainsaw, we saw what we'd missed on our first pass: sawdust on the pavement and the remains of a tree that had been cut back from where it had fallen across the trail. The old fellow was hauling the wood he'd cut from the fallen tree. He'd simply been an old man struggling under a heavy load he may have needed to heat his home during that cold New Hampshire winter.

Just like that, our story was torn asunder and exposed for what it was: a mix of fact and fiction we interwove as we went along.

Our conflict stories need the same rending, the same exposure for what they really are: something we partly make up, a mix of fact and fiction to which we grow increasingly committed the more we tell the story to ourselves and others.

Humans are natural storytellers. We tell stories to communicate and connect, entertain and educate, persuade and inspire, unite and divide, appreciate and demonize. Stories help us retain ideas and try new ones on for size. We use stories to understand and make meaning, constructing our world with their help. Australian psychologist Peter O'Connor says, "Not to have a story is in fact not to be human."[1]

Stories are part of the fabric of our lives from the beginning. We come to life, as writer Paul Elie says, in the middle of stories that are not ours.[2] And we hear and learn stories from our earliest years, stories from our family and friends, stories from our schools and places of worship, stories from our books and movies.

When I was very little, my mother wove stories for me every night at bedtime, using a little ceramic cottage as the launching point for each tale. The cottage had a light inside from the type of bulb that comes on Christmas tree lights, and together we would peer in to see the ceramic wolf in Grandma's bed, Red Riding Hood nearby, a basket of goodies on her arm. In my mother's stories, the wolf and Little Red had many adventures together, usually with other forest creatures, and the stories never involved the wolf eating anyone. I recall being very excited to hear each night's story and to this day fondly remember the happiness and security I felt staring into that little cottage while my mother sat next to me. It is one of my most treasured memories of my mother, who died while I was in my midtwenties. I still have the ceramic cottage, I still have a soft spot for animals, and I still have a very favorable view of wolves. My mother's bedtime stories shaped my opinions before I knew I had any.

Stories about our conflicts are also part of the fabric of our lives. We tell those stories to ourselves on our morning run, while we mow the lawn, and in the middle of the night as we chase sleep. We tell them to others in order to get support and vindication, be told we're reasonable, help us think, and feel better. We may not recognize them as stories, yet that is what they are.

As we tell these stories, they begin to develop a shape. They shift and change as we emphasize some parts of what happened, leave out other parts, and add interpretation, diagnosis, and judgment. They morph as we filter what happened through the screens of our values and beliefs, perceptions and assumptions. They change from what a videotape might have captured because we did not—could not—notice and retain every detail. As such, they are not full testaments to what happened. American novelist Joan Didion famously said, "We tell ourselves stories in order to live…We look for the sermon in the suicide, for the social or moral lesson in the murder of five. We interpret what we see, select the most workable of the multiple choices."[3]

Over time, with more telling, our stories begin to shine a bit from the polishing they're receiving. We are, though we don't call it this, practicing our stories. We are rehearsing them. And as we rehearse, our stories begin to harden into something that feels certain and true. In conflicts that are difficult and feeling stuck, we are approaching danger as we harden our stories, but we are usually not aware of this. We feel quite the opposite: we experience an odd relief from our stories, perhaps because they give us the comfort of familiarity even while they also give us the discomfort of unresolved tension.

Our Conflict Stories Shape Our Conflicts

Imagine this: You're standing at the edge of dense woods. The woods are filled with briars, tree roots sticking up from the soil, and low-hanging branches. On the other side of the woods is a sunny meadow filled with wildflowers, but you can barely make it out through the thick woods.

I ask you to get yourself to that sunny meadow as fast as you can. You have two choices for proceeding: one is to bushwhack through the woods I just described; the other is to take a well-worn footpath that leads to the meadow. Both are about the same distance. Which should you choose, given my request that you hurry? I am not trying to trick you; the right answer is the well-worn path. It's easier. It's faster. It's more efficient.

Now imagine this: I ask you to get yourself to the sunny meadow, without benefit of the well-worn path. I ask you to do this every day for a while. You traverse the same section of woods again and again, back and forth. What happens? You create a new well-worn path. The more you use it, the more worn it becomes. It gets easier, faster, and more efficient. Given enough time the old path, unused, grows over.

Neural pathways in your brain—think of them as mental shortcuts—are created in ways similar to that well-worn path. If you learned to count or to multiply in the way I did, you learned by repetition. Perhaps your parents proudly asked you to count to ten for everyone you saw so you could show off your new skill. Maybe your teacher made a memorization game out of the multiplication tables, like mine did. You practiced and practiced and eventually you didn't need to think about it when someone asked you the product of four times four.

Your conflict stories work similarly. The more you rehearse a story by telling it over and over again, the stronger the mental shortcut becomes. Tell your story enough and you start to feel as certain about it as you do that four times four is sixteen. You begin to see your story as The Truth.

Repetition doesn't just strengthen a memory; it also increases persuasiveness.[4] "There is nothing so absurd that it cannot be believed as truth if repeated often enough," philosopher William James warned us over a century ago. How right he turned out to be. Repetition of a message increases its persuasiveness, insight not lost on politicians and ad agencies. When we're exposed to a statement repeated even just once, we are more inclined to believe the statement is true.[5] And when we recollect a story in our minds, that act causes us to reexperience it, increasing our fluency with it and adding to its persuasive effect, as though it had been repeated twice.[6] We are, in effect, persuading ourselves more each time we retell our story.

Well-told stories transport us inside the story and influence our beliefs. The more engaging the story and the more vivid the imagery, the greater the effect. Transportation by vivid narrative, as it's called, can be so strong that even in studies where the story was clearly labeled as fiction, real-world beliefs were influenced by the story.[7] So, our stories shape our opinions, though we tend to think it's the other way around. Our conflict stories shape our opinions about the conflict and the way, then, we respond.

The way other people react to our conflict stories also shapes our conflicts. A friend was regaling me with a story about a court employee who treated her with disrespect. As I listened to her description of the employee's behavior, I felt outrage on my friend's behalf. I heard myself say, "That's just not acceptable! How could she think it's ok to treat you that way?" I watched my friend grow increasingly more incensed as she told the story and as I supported her by endorsing her outrage. With my outrage I was contributing to the construct of her conflict story about this employee; I was inadvertently contributing to the shape of her newly born stuck story.

Instead, what if I had said something like, "Oh my. Do you think she must have been having a terrible day to have said something like that?" Or, "Yikes! You sure can be a force to be reckoned with when someone inadvertently steps on your toes." Instead of endorsing a story already taking shape with gusto, I could have chosen to help my friend consider additional ways of looking at her experience. Who knows whether those ways would have been useful or helpful to her? I tell you this experience simply to highlight that the way we support someone who entrusts us with their conflict story has an impact, even if we do not intend that to be so.

Constructing stories about our conflicts may be a natural thing to do, yet if we are unconscious of the ways our stories influence our conflicts, we risk getting stuck in them. After learning about stuck stories, one of my graduate students, Adele, wrote in a paper, "It is crucial for me to examine the way I have distorted the conversation to serve my views of myself."

Our Conflict Stories Are Not Accurate

Consider this: What were you doing the moment you heard about the passenger jets hitting the World Trade Center in New York on September 11, 2001? What did you do in the minutes and hours afterward?

I was in my office at the Vermont college where I directed a conflict management degree program. My colleague Wayne tapped on my office door and said, "I don't really know for sure what's going on, but there are some reports about a plane hitting the World Trade Center."

"Oh no!" I gasped. "I remember seeing pictures of the plane that hit the Empire State Building in the 1940s. It was awful." I tried to load CNN's homepage on my laptop. It wouldn't load. We thought that a lot of people must be trying to get onto the website. We sat and waited, worrying about what might have happened to the pilot and the people on the floor he hit.

Finally, a photo loaded: the two World Trade Center towers, one burning, with a passenger jet in the air nearby. "Gee," I said to Wayne, "that must be an optical illusion because a passenger jet can't possibly be as close to the World Trade Center as it looks. The flight corridor isn't anywhere near there." My mind could not yet fathom that anything but an errant single-engine plane could have hit the first tower.

My memories of that day are very vivid and still cause my stomach to lurch when I recall them. I remember the moment I finally understood that this was not pilot error with a small plane. I remember frantically trying to reach my brother in Tribeca, a New York neighborhood not far from the towers, and getting repeated "all circuits are busy" messages. I remember calling my husband at his faculty office two states away because I desperately needed just to hear his voice. I remember rolling a television cart into the main section of the library and sitting for hours there with colleagues and students, many of us crying as events unfolded on the screen before us. I remember calling my sister and learning that my brother's wife and baby were on a plane that took off around the time the first plane hit the tower. I remember sobbing when I saw that people were jumping from the towers; those images are seared on my brain and still bring instant tears when I recall them. I remember being unable to register that the first tower had actually collapsed, even as I watched the live broadcast of it happening.

I feel sure of those memories. You may well feel sure of your vivid memories of that day, too. We should not feel quite so sure.

Cognitive psychologist Daniel Simons also has a vivid memory from that day, a memory he felt certain about. But when he e-mailed those who had been with him in his office the moment he heard the news, their memories of who'd brought the news and what they each did differed in some very important ways from Simons's recollections. He realized that his very clear memories were not accurate, despite the vividness of them.

Simons's recounting of his mistaken memory caused me to read my journal entry from September 12, 2001. I had not read it since I wrote it. Some parts of the vivid and emotionally powerful recollections I shared above turned out to be quite incorrect. Even though I was very sure of my memories from that day, mine were no more accurate than Simons's were.

His memory—my memory, your memory—of that day is not accurate because what is stored in memory is not an exact replica of reality, but a re-creation of it. Though it's been said for years that memory is like a video recording we can play back, it turns out the metaphor is flawed. Each time we recall a memory, we combine details we *do* remember with our expectations for what we *should* remember. The revised memory then gets stored, and it is that revised memory we recall next time. And so on. The longer the time between an event and its recollection, the greater the inaccuracy. It would be more useful, then, to think of memory like a perpetually edited video that shares only some data with the original recording

When something momentous happens, we often try to make meaning of it by talking to others and gauging their reactions, says Avril Thorne, a psychologist studying narrative memory at the University of California at Santa Cruz. The feedback we receive from their reactions then shapes our future memories of what transpired. The editing continues.

Vivid memories feel more accurate, but they aren't more accurate. The strong, vivid recollection of very emotional memories, like the ones many of us in the United States have of 9/11, are just as likely to be inaccurate as ordinary memories are. Yet we don't want to believe it; we believe those memories are more accurate because they *feel* so vivid. Our emotions affect how we think we remember, even if they do not affect how much we actually remember. "Unfortunately, people regularly use vividness and emotionality as an indicator of accuracy; they use these cues to assess how confident they are in a memory,"[8] say Simons and his coauthor, Christopher Chabris.

So you can see that your conflict stories are very powerful indeed. You see the result of their influence in the actions you take as the conflict continues, in the beliefs you adopt about the other person, and in the certainty you feel about what happened. You may also see your conflict stories' power in the person you have become. Psychologist Jeremy Dean proposes that we effectively create ourselves by choosing which memories to recall.[9] I find this idea compelling and it makes me ask, *By committing to the conflict story you have rehearsed and made a powerful memory, is that part of the self you wish to create?*

Stuck Stories

A woman told me a story about her brother, with whom she'd experienced ongoing tension since their father's dementia finally necessitated twenty-four-hour care. Her father's care had "fallen on her shoulders," Linda said, while her brother "went off and played." Her father now lived with her, and she had taken a leave from work to care for him. Meanwhile, her brother's work had him traveling the world and visiting exotic locales. After trying unsuccessfully for many months to persuade her brother to help care for their father, she asked me to help her figure out how to persuade him.

I asked her why persuading him to help was the goal she most wanted to achieve. She spoke of valuing family, of fairness and equity, and of "doing the right thing" by their father, a World War II vet who had done so much for his country and his family. She spoke of her playboy brother who never shouldered adult responsibility and of her frustration that her brother knew she'd simply suffer and do it all by herself. She said she'd always been "the responsible one" and her brother "the playboy one," and that she was tired of playing the role relegated to her since childhood.

She told me of the most recent telephone conversation with her brother, in which he deftly thwarted her attempts to get him to visit, repeatedly used the excuse that his business travel would prevent him from coming, and denied her accusations that he did not love their father enough. It was, she said, a conversation she'd replayed in her mind many times, trying to figure out what she could have said differently to change the outcome. She told me that every telephone conversation with her brother now unfolded similarly, and this one "went exactly as I knew it would. He never changes."

Linda had a very well rehearsed stuck story about her brother and the conflict they faced together. In the first chapter I said that Stuck Stories are like a movie trailer, a montage of the moments most compelling to you (and perhaps the ones you want others to be most compelled by, too), certain scenes amplified and others left on the cutting room floor. A stuck story should never be taken at face value, because it is a construction, a tapestry woven of accurate and inaccurate recollections, events included because they were powerful in some way to you, interpretations filtered through your values, judgments, beliefs, perceptions, and assumptions. When you act on your stuck story as though it is *the* story of the conflict, you are tricking yourself.

All this is not to say that your stuck story is unimportant. On the contrary, it helps you shine a light into the darkness. U2 front man and social justice activist Bono has been quoted as saying, "Whenever you see darkness, there is extraordinary opportunity for the light to burn brighter." Like turning on the light inside the little ceramic cottage from my childhood, you can choose to shine light on your own conflict story and finally see what it's been trying to tell you all along.

First you must stop confusing your stuck story with The Truth. Whenever I teach my Interpersonal Conflict Resolution course, on the first day of class I write on the board that famous quote often attributed to Anaïs Nin and perhaps with origins in the Talmud: "We don't see things as they are. We see things as we are."[10]

After you learn to stop confusing your stuck story with The Truth, you must then sever your attachment to that story. This is usually not easy because your mind tells you it's a good and right story. The Dalai Lama has said, "Most of our troubles are due to our passionate desire for and attachment to things that we misapprehend as enduring entities."[11] When you are committed to your stuck story, you make it an enduring entity by feeding it through repetition. You can choose to stop feeding it and sever your dependence upon it.

You can begin by ceasing to rehearse it, by ceasing to tell it to yourself or others. If your stuck story is one that has been with you for a while, and your mind may be used to telling the story, this may feel like a difficult invitation to carry out. Shortly, I'll introduce you to something you can do instead, to help fill the vacuum created by ceasing to practice your stuck story. In the meantime, try allowing yourself to consider the idea of abandoning it for something better. Begin to prepare yourself for letting it go.

Thomas Moore wrote, "You don't have to write a book, but you can tell your story, again and again. Over time, you may tell it more effectively, and its sheer beauty will help you and connect you to the people in your life."[12] He suggests that the repeated telling of a story gradually allows the pieces of life experience to find their relation to each other. I quite agree with this idea. Your stuck story is something to love even while releasing it, because the polishing you've given it will help you notice great insight when you are ready to look for it.

I invited Linda to stop rehearsing the story about her inconsiderate brother and about the heavy burden she faced. In doing so I was not suggesting that she pretend she wasn't frustrated or that she wasn't working very hard to care for her father; this practice is not about pretending reality does not exist. It is about allowing a fuller version of reality to become available to you.

I invited Linda to stop talking about her stuck story with friends. I told her that soon I would ask her to stop telling versions of it to me, too. Together, we came up with a plan that each time she observed herself beginning to ruminate on her stuck story, she would sing a song instead. I know that sounds silly. But Linda enjoyed singing and had done musical theater in her community. The idea was to keep her mind from its stuck story habit and distract it by doing something else instead, for now. If she ever decided that her stuck story was the best thing to hold on to, that story was certainly not going anywhere and she could readopt it then. Our goal was, for a time, to prevent her stuck story from hardening more as a result of ongoing rehearsal.

When we spoke next, she was both aghast and full of good humor. "I've never sung so many show tunes!" she laughed. But beneath the laughter, she was startled to notice how much of her mental energy had been going to her conflict story. This was not what she wanted for her life or for her father's final years.

Now, you may be thinking that you do not spend nearly the time she did dwelling on your own stuck story.

Are you sure? How much is too much? Is the time you spend on it time you can get back? When you are old and getting ready to leave this world, is it time you will be glad you spent?

A very good way to sever attachment to your stuck story is to begin trying to understand what the story is really trying to tell you about yourself—to look beneath the story for the meaning. This is the essence of the first pivot: to stop being a victim of your stuck story and attend instead to the meaning it is trying to communicate to you.

Don't make the mistake of asking yourself what the story is trying to tell you about the other person. Your mind may seize this opportunity to rehearse another story, a parallel one, as it tries to soothe and care-take you. The conflict pivot practice is all about you. I am not saying that the other person never figures into it; I am saying that you must work with yourself first.

You must also avoid the temptation to be hamstrung by the "facts" in your stuck story. These "facts" are distorted by your flawed human memory. And you would do well to treat fact as illusion, to loosen your death grip on the rational and objective, to understand that rationality is not pure and objectivity is colored by who and how you are in the world. Moore says it well: "Fact is an illusion, because every fact is part of a story and is riddled with imagination. Imagination is real because every perception of the world around us is absolutely colored by the narrative or image-filled lens through which we perceive. We are all poets and artists as we live our daily lives, whether or not we recognize this role and whether or not we believe it."[13]

So let us be poets and artists living our daily lives. We do this, in part, by attending to what matters.

This is what doesn't matter:

- the degree to which your stuck conflict story is true
- how much of your memory about what happened is accurate
- The Truth about What Happened
- that others see the same flaws you do in your conflict partner
- that others agree with you or have had the same experience with him or her

Don't spend an ounce more of your energy on any of these. They are trapping you.

This is what matters:

- the reality your story creates for you,[14] the story-maker
- the meaning you make with your story
- giving your story credence without giving it power over you
- pivoting away from just telling your stuck story and pivoting toward its meaning

Working with the Pivot 1 Questions

The summer before I left for college, I had the very good fortune to spend a week with Isaac Asimov, Isadore Adler, and other luminaries at The Rensselaerville Institute, then known as the Institute on Man and Science. Each summer the institute brought together experts on space, science, history, philosophy, and medicine to consider a wide range of social issues facing humankind. That summer, the institute included a small group of students in the think tank.

The think tank's task was this: Imagine that we've made contact with extraterrestrial life. How should the public be told in order to prevent mass chaos? While my sixteen-year-old self didn't realize it at the time, that memorable week watching, learning from, and talking with these brilliant thinkers was a first step I took in what ultimately became my career in conflict resolution. Contemplating how to communicate effectively, manage fear and change, and embrace possibility are, after all, key elements of my work today.

Isaac Asimov was one of the first people to teach me how to think expansively and to cultivate my curiosity instead of my judgment (which, frankly, didn't need a great deal more cultivation). In my diary from that summer, I wrote something he told the group of us one day at lunch:

> People always think scientists love the "Eureka!" moment. "Eureka!" is fun, yes. But I prefer "Hmmm, that's interesting…" because that gets us on the trail of a new discovery.

This is the attitude I invite you to bring to the Pivot 1 questions. These questions are not the place to judge yourself, your thinking, or your reactions to the conflict. If anything, the Pivot 1 questions are the place to be gentle and kind to yourself, because you're setting a foundation for Pivot 2, a foundation you'll use to create your own "Hmmm, that's interesting…" moment.

The Pivot 1 questions should not be considered sequential; the questions do not build on each other.

Pivot 1 is about looking at your stuck story from a variety of angles, turning it over in your mind like you might turn over an interesting gemstone in your hands, noticing different things about it as you look at the many facets. Each question is asked in that spirit, and your answers will serve as reference points later on.

Don't skip any questions. If, at first, you can't come up with an answer to a question, allow yourself time to ponder. This is not a race to the finish. Go for a walk or play with your dog, allowing the question to hover in your mind. Stretch out in a sunbeam and breathe deeply, meditating on the question. See what comes up.

Worksheet Question 1
Who is the tension or conflict with and what is it about?

Don't overthink the second part of this question; just write and keep it simple.

Worksheet Question 2
To what have you reacted most strongly in the conflict?

Consider which moments in the conflict have made you react most strongly. Think about things the other person said that really got your goat. Recall the things he or she did that got under your skin, maybe made your heart pound more rapidly or caused you to clench your jaw in order to stop yourself from saying things you dearly wanted to say. Maybe you went ahead and said them.

The ways a strong reaction manifests itself are as varied as people are varied. Some people, like my Midwestern husband, show strong reaction by going very silent and very still. Others, like me, start using emphatic gestures and our voice volume goes up a notch. Some people storm out, some cross their arms, some freeze, some start to shake with held-in fury. Some people cough or feel their airways constrict. Still others interrupt and overtake the airspace.

So, you may be able to identify a strong reaction by the way your body responds or by the degree of anger or pain you experience. These are good places to start your inquiry.

Here are the kinds of things people have told me made them react most strongly. They won't necessarily be things that bother you (there's a reason for that and we'll talk about it in the second pivot), but I hope they will give you a sense of what this question is asking of you.

- I reacted most strongly to the suggestion that, once again, I have to be the one to give up my career so he can do what he wants.
- I reacted most strongly to her getting up and walking from the room, as though I had been dismissed and she had better things to do.
- I have reacted most strongly to the suggestion that I'm not working as hard as others in my department.
- I reacted most strongly to hearing she was telling others that we downsized our house because we couldn't afford the larger home.
- I have reacted most strongly to being told my house is a pigsty.

- I have reacted most strongly to his sexist jokes.

If we return to the situation Linda faced with her ailing father and apparently unhelpful brother, we can see that she reacted strongly to the disregard she felt from her brother. She also reacted strongly to the disregard she believed her brother had for their father; you might say that she was angry on her father's behalf. She said to me, "I am trapped by my brother and by my father's circumstances. I am trapped and I am alone, doing it all. I hate that I've shown anger toward my dad that I know is really misplaced anger at my brother's disregard for us."

Do you notice how Linda has turned from an examination of her brother's faults to a reflection about herself and how she's experiencing the conflict? This is what you want to achieve with the Pivot 1 questions, too. They are about you; don't let yourself off the hook by spending your energy considering the other person's flaws, as that's a thinking muscle that is likely already well developed. When I am teaching graduate students or leading a corporate training, I say, "Let's not come in here and practice doing more of what you already know how to do. That's not learning. It's performing. Let's stretch and strengthen unused muscles in a space like this where it's safe not to get it perfect right away."

Worksheet Question 3
When you tell your story of the conflict to others or yourself, what do you focus on most?

This question is about identifying the parts of your stuck story that most lure you into their clutches, the parts of the conflict that probably have a most important message for you.

Sit back and run through your stuck story again in your mind. Try to recall the way you may have told the story to others. What did you tell them? What parts did you emphasize? Try to recall the parts of the conflict that you have mused over repeatedly. What parts do you keep returning to? What troubles you when you awake at 2:00 a.m.? What do you ponder while on the treadmill?

Go ahead, tell your stuck story out loud. Hearing yourself tell it may help you notice things you don't notice when you keep it only in your head. If your tone of voice isn't too angry, your baby or your dog might be very happy to listen to your story.

Clients have told me they dwell on the following kinds of things most. Again, these may not be at all like what you dwell on, but are intended to give you a better sense of what this question is asking you to uncover:

- I dwell on how he simply dismisses me when he doesn't want to talk about what's on my mind.
- I dwell on the way he made me feel like an idiot in front of others.
- I dwell on her comment that I'm "new money."
- I dwell on how I couldn't find the right retort to put him in his place.
- I dwell on how she's always telling me what to do and wants to control everything.
- I dwell on how he blames me for what's wrong in the relationship.
- I dwell on being told I'm not a devout enough Christian for their family.
- I dwell on how unjust it is to insult my housekeeping when she knows I work full-time,

am raising two children alone, and never have a moment to myself.

- I dwell on the implication that women don't measure up to men in management jobs.

My client with the jet-setting brother and elderly father did not have difficulty identifying what she dwells on most. Her movie trailer, her stuck story, revealed it with well-polished gusto: her brother's disregard and the loneliness she felt in carrying a responsibility she did not want to experience as a burden.

If it's not obvious to you right away what you dwell on most, give yourself time. Allow your stuck story to bubble to the surface and notice what comes up most frequently. Don't worry about interpretation yet; focus on what's snagged you. Don't go on to the second pivot until you can see what's most hooked your attention.

If you are tempted to hurry past this step and toward interpretation, remember this apple cart story: A farmer headed down a bumpy, pothole-ridden dirt road with a cart filled to the brim with freshly picked apples. Passing a gentleman headed in the other direction, he asked, "How long will it take me to get to market headed this way?" The other fellow looked at the cart full of apples, then down at the muddy potholes. "An hour if you go slowly," he replied, "and all day if you go fast."

Your mind may try to thwart you. Persevere. Instead of pushing the discomfort away, allow yourself to feel it. Step closer to it. Look for the meaning in it.

Your Emotional State during Pivot 1

Now, I recognize that I am asking you to relive your

conflict and ruminate on your stuck story, even after making the case that your stuck story is a problem. I will be asking you to move past your stuck story soon enough, but first it is important to mine it for what it's really worth.

There is a downside to the first pivot: you may reexperience some of the anger, frustration, and pain of the conflict. Most people experience just a mild frustration, and it is nothing to worry about. Occasionally, people who have very strong anger about their conflict can feel escalated again after reconsidering their stuck story (another good reason to let go of a stuck story). If that is your tendency, here are a few things to keep in mind as you finish Pivot 1.

First, ruminating about a conflict can trigger displaced aggression.[15] For instance, if you have just finished with the Pivot 1 questions and you hear your wife's car pulling into the garage as she returns home from work, beware of stomping into the kitchen and barking something like, "You said you'd be home an hour ago and now I'm late for the gym!" If you have just been angered by something else, that is really what still angers you, not your wife's arrival time. She just happens to be, unfortunately for her, the person standing in front of you right now.

Second, if you tend toward anger that is very strong and stormy, the worst thing you can do right now is continue to focus on your hurt and angry feelings after finishing the Pivot 1 questions. Dr. Brad Bushman, who has done quite a bit of research on anger, venting, and the ways people communicate when angry, tells us that, when angry, if you focus too much on how you're feeling, it usually backfires and makes you more aggressive.[16]

A better approach is to spend a few minutes now taking what Bushman and colleagues call a "self-distancing perspective." The idea is to move away from a situation to a point where you can watch the event unfold from a distance. It can help you calm down.

Stephen Shick, a Unitarian Universalist minister who took one of my graduate courses, shared a lovely meditation he uses in tense moments. Shick had a colleague who was fond of putting a present moment into perspective by comparing it to well-known historical moments. The colleague would say things like, "We are in the same moment as the Union Army was at Gettysburg right before the reinforcements arrived." Shick built on that idea to create this excellent example of taking a self-distancing perspective:

> I began practicing viewing my own life as a historian might. When I felt particularly stressful I would get up from my desk, walk to the corner of the room, and watch myself at work. Often I would find myself laughing fondly at the man hunched tensely over his desk. Then I would briefly narrate the situation. This little exercise helped me to step outside of my self-centered view of the world. In our troubled world I am finding more need to be a disciplined observer of my own life.[17]

This practice isn't only helpful if you're feeling anger after Pivot 1; it's a useful practice anytime you're feeling hot under the collar.

Another useful choice would be to move on immediately to Pivot 2, a pivot that helps you interpret the message your anger is giving you. I have found that when I'm angry and feeling stuck, the second pivot helps me enormously.

4

THE SECOND PIVOT

Pivot Away from Their Behavior and Toward Your Hooks

We had just moved from the Burlington, Vermont, area to a small town in New Hampshire. The move had been a whirlwind, our Vermont house selling in a matter of days, far faster than we anticipated, and resulting in a new house purchased quickly, a moving van scheduled in a narrow window, and a mad rush to sift and pack a lifetime of belongings.

The day after we moved, I pulled into a local Mobil station to fill up. The light that signals a near-empty gas tank glared at me from my dashboard; that's something I rarely let happen. I reached for my wallet and realized I had left it at the new house. I chalked it up to the frenzy of the move.

Fortunately, I had a Mobil Speedpass, a little plastic gizmo that attached to my keychain and allowed me to pump gas while automatically deducting the amount from my checking account. I got out and waved the Speedpass at the designated spot on the gas pump, waiting for the signal light to show me the pump recognized it and I was good to go. The light didn't come on. I waved the gizmo some more. No light. I ran it over the spot again, trying different angles. No light.

I walked into the gas station and up to the counter. "Hi there. I'm having a little trouble with my Speedpass. I can't get it to work at the pump. Can you help me?" I said.

The clerk pursed his lips in a little frown of disapproval, not unlike *Saturday Night Live's* Church Lady. "It was working a few minutes ago," he said under his breath, slightly shaking his head back and forth at my ineptness.

I noticed my own lips pursing in disapproval now, too. I was perfectly capable of properly waving a tiny piece of plastic at a gas pump. My teeth threatened to start gnashing.

Now, I'm from New York originally. I may have lived in northern New England my entire adult life, but New York blood still courses through my veins. Sarcasm comes naturally to me, though I've learned to bite my tongue and temper myself in the less in-your-face north country. Most of the time. It's harder to do when I'm under stress, as I had been due to this overnight relocation.

Upon hearing the clerk's response, Bad Tammy woke up inside my head, ready to fight. She wanted to say, very exaggeratedly for the most sarcastic effect, "Oh, I see, customer service is your strength." She also mumbled something about People from New Hampshire, which I refused to acknowledge because I was now People from New Hampshire.

Bad Tammy opened my mouth, but, thankfully, Good Tammy took over in the nick of time. Good Tammy said, "What do you mean?"

The clerk looked at me and shook his head again. "I'm sorry," he said, "The pump's been doing that off and on for days, but the manager doesn't believe there's a problem. That's because when he looks at it, it's working. The pump's playing cat and mouse. I bet when we go out there now, it'll be working. Damn thing is driving me crazy."

Good Tammy turned and shot a triumphant look at Bad Tammy. See, she said to Bad Tammy, you almost got us into trouble for nothing. It wasn't about us at all. That clerk was shaking his head at his own problems and his own frustrations, not at our stupidity. Bad Tammy rolled her eyes, turned her back on us, and went back to sleep.

The Speedpass and pump worked just fine when the clerk and I went outside together. Instead of peeling out guns blazing, I drove away smiling with satisfaction. Instead of driving away and beating myself up for unkind behavior, I drove away feeling good that I was able to walk the talk this time. Instead of driving away unable to show my face at that Mobil station again, I drove away with a new acquaintance.

That's the magic of knowing your conflict hooks and how to handle them: some conflict will disappear entirely from your life. And for the conflict that remains, you will not only be able to dramatically improve your reaction, but you will gain clarity about the conflict's true nature.

Getting Unhooked from a Conflict

Getting unhooked from a conflict is not unlike

freeing yourself from a barbed wire fence. There you are, squeezing between two rows of barbed wire, on your way to reaching a beautiful flower you wish to photograph, and the wool sweater your grandmother lovingly knitted you inadvertently becomes snagged. You are thwarted in your attempt to continue on. There is no going forward until you free yourself.

You're familiar with hooks: hooks for hanging coats, hooks for fishing, hooks for crocheting, hooks in computer programming, hooks in barbed wire. They share a kindred function: to catch and hold.

When it's barbed wire, you know that continuing to pull will only result in damage. Your beloved sweater will be ruined, or worse, you will render yourself bloody when the barb snags your skin. Instead, you must attend to the hook. You must lessen your distance from it to gain your freedom. You must stop pulling and tugging and move closer to the hook so that you have wiggle room to free your sweater's fibers. It can be tricky to achieve, even require a contortionist's skill the first time, but with commitment you can achieve your freedom without damage to something you love.

It's similar in conflict. There you are, going about your business, and suddenly, something hooks you. It grabs your attention, probably not in a good way. Because there's a person in front of you the moment you're hooked, you erroneously suppose he or she is the cause, like the dog who seemed to blame my friend for the pain in his back. Blame is like that, so tempting, so easy. But that would be like blaming the flower in the field.

To unhook yourself from a conflict in a real and useful way, you must learn what hooks you, why it hooks you, and how to manage your hooks when you become snagged. Initially, you may find this undertaking a bit uncomfortable, though that discomfort transforms into something very freeing once you ferret out your hooks. As you become familiar with the practice, you will begin to view your discomfort not as something to avoid, but as an ally you readily welcome.

When It's Not The Other Person

Picture yourself stepping out onto the Capilano Canyon Bridge, a suspension bridge in Vancouver, British Columbia. The Capilano Canyon Bridge is 230 feet high, 450 feet long, and sways in the breeze. Picture yourself walking across this swaying bridge. If you're like most people, walking across the bridge will produce real anxiety.

Now imagine that, just as you pass the midpoint in the bridge, when your anxiety is about at its peak, an attractive person of the gender toward which you're romantically inclined asks you if you'd be willing to stop for a brief survey. After you're done, they tell you they'd be happy to discuss the study further if you want to call that evening. The survey taker tears off a corner of the paper, writes down his or her phone number, and hands it to you. Do you call?

In 1974, psychologists Art Aron and Donald Dutton posted a female on the bridge, and she approached male bridge-crossers with her questionnaire (the survey was a red herring, of course; its purpose was solely to engage the men initially and cause them to pause partway across the bridge). They found that about 50 percent of the participants did call the survey taker in their classic experiment.[1] But when they repeated the experiment on a wide sturdy bridge that was just a few feet off the ground, only 12.5 percent called. In this and a series of related experiments, they showed that when we're in a heightened state of arousal, we naturally seek out context to explain that heightened emotion. In the process we can mistake the true source of that arousal. It's called misattribution of arousal.

In an argument, misattribution of arousal may cause you to associate the other person with your heightened state of anger. Or perhaps he or she blames you. Just like on the bridge, your brain is searching for context. You look around and what do you see as the source of all this emotional arousal? The person in front of you, damn them.

But odds are good that they are not the true cause of your discomfort or suffering. To find that cause, you must first embrace the discomfort. To paraphrase Jung, everything that irritates you about others can lead you to an understanding of yourself.[2]

Discomfort Is Your Ally

Freedom from a conflict doesn't come from pushing discomfort away. Freedom from a conflict comes from drawing closer to it, from becoming intimate with it, from staying present with it, and allowing it to teach you. Psychologist Jeffrey Kottler, who has written very meaningfully about the subject of uncovering what hooks you in conflict, says that if the goal is to change a long-standing pattern, discomfort may be your greatest ally.[3]

To capitalize on your discomfort, you may have to resist a long-held habit of pushing discomfort away. Dr. Mark Epstein tells the story of a man seeking therapy in order to rid himself of emotional pain plaguing him since his divorce. Instead of trying to push the pain away, Epstein invites him to stay with the pain and allow himself to feel it more intensely. He teaches the man to meditate so that he can learn what it means to stay present with an experience. While meditating one day, the man notices an itch develop. Instead of trying to ignore it, or push it away, or judge it as unwanted, he chooses to watch the itch develop and crest, then disappear without needing to scratch it. In that pivotal moment, the man understands what his therapist meant by encouraging him to stay with his emotional state, and his depression and emotional pain finally begin to shift. Epstein says, "His feelings began to change only when he dropped the desire to change them."[4]

To make discomfort your ally, try allowing yourself to take your conflict very personally for a bit of time. I do sometimes hear people say that the best way to deal with conflict is not to take it personally. It is not bad advice because, as don Miguel Ruiz has reminded us, "Nothing others do is because of you. What others say and do is a projection of their own reality."[5] Yet, it can be quite impossible advice to implement. That's because there's something else you have to do first, before you can hope to stop taking it personally: you have to take it *more* personally. Conflict by its very nature lives in our guts and chews on our insides; it is personal in some ways.

So, to learn how not to take it personally, you must first step closer to it, wrap your arms around it, accept it, and work with it. You must understand why it's eating at you. A little later in this chapter, I will share some ways you can explore and discover the message your discomfort is sending.

To make discomfort your ally, you may also need to allow yourself to fully experience the anger you feel. I hear a lot about "anger management" these days; it has become fashionable, as though it is not all right to feel anger fully. Now, of course there is a difference between allowing yourself to experience your anger fully and acting on that anger in a way that inflicts damage on another. I am not suggesting the latter. I am suggesting that your anger is trying to tell you something so very important and that to push it away as a "bad" emotion is a mistake.

Buddhist monk and teacher Thích Nhất Hạnh says that you need to cook anger in order to use it well, much like you must cook raw potatoes before you can eat them. If you know how to cook the raw energy of your anger, you can transform it into positive energy: "Embrace your anger with a lot of tenderness. Your anger is not your enemy, your anger is your baby."[6]

Allow your anger to wash over you. Note its texture, its taste, the way it lives in your body. Instead of rejecting it, cradle it in your arms and ask your anger, "What are you trying to tell me?"

Benefits of Knowing Your Conflict Hooks

Familiarity with your conflict hooks, combined with knowing how to manage them, will help you navigate conflict with greater balance and calm. I can tell you from personal experience that you will not always successfully remain balanced even when you know your hooks, but you will be able to increase the frequency with which you retain your stability and equilibrium. There is an old story that speaks to the power you have when you can keep your balance in the face of a storm:

There was once an old man known for being able to

defeat any challenger. His reputation extended throughout the land and many gathered to study under him. One day a young warrior arrived at the old man's village. He was determined to be the first to defeat the great master, since he had both strength and the ability to notice and exploit an opponent's weakness.

The old master gladly accepted the young warrior's challenge. As the two faced one another, the young warrior began to hurl insults at the old master. The verbal insults went on for hours, yet the old master merely stood there motionless and calm. Finally, the young warrior exhausted himself. Defeated, he left.

The great master's students gathered around the old man. "How could you endure such an indignity?" they wondered. "And how were you able to drive him away?"

"If someone comes to give you a gift and you do not receive it," the master replied, "to whom does the gift belong?"

Knowing and being able to manage your conflict hooks enables you not to accept gifts like the ones the great master was offered. Awareness of your conflict hooks will also allow you to notice that some conflict isn't conflict at all, that not all conflict you perceive is true conflict. This awareness will be like your own personal Mobil station moment, when you recognize a false alarm when you see one.

Tibetan Buddhist teacher Tsoknyi Rinpoche had a frightening midflight experience over Nepal, one that left many on the plane screaming and crying out of fear for their lives. The experience left him with what he calls "residual fear" on later flights. He says, "The fear I felt on that return trip…and the fear I felt for many years later, even when I was traveling on large commercial airliners was real, in the sense that I was fully experiencing it.

However, as I looked back on each subsequent experience, I had to admit that it wasn't true. That is, it wasn't grounded in actual, present circumstances, but instead was triggered by residual memories of a past experience."[7] Rinpoche uses a simple, four-word mantra to help ground him in such moments: *real but not true*.

When you are in chronic conflict with someone, you may let the residual memory of your past experiences with this person trigger your reaction, even when the actual, present circumstances, do not necessarily call upon you to react in that way. Sometimes, the conflict you're experiencing is real but not true. In other words, your thoughts and feelings are real, but they may not be accurate reflections of what is happening right now. Knowing your hooks can help you navigate such moments and differentiate real from true.

Experience with your conflict hooks will help you understand why certain things that bother you do not bother others, and why something that bothers someone else does not bother you. Your hooks are your own. When people say to you, "It's no big deal; let it go," it is very possible that they don't share your hooks. I suspect that when their own hooks snag them, they may not so easily be able to follow their own advice.

Knowing your conflict hooks will also help you refrain from the seduction of blaming. One way to understand the act of blaming is to see it as a way to push your discomfort away from you, to dodge your own anxieties. In the film *The Interpreter,* Nicole Kidman's character, Silvia Broome, said, "Vengeance is a lazy form of grief." Blame is a lazy form of self-preservation, one you may use to avoid the harder—yet much more fulfilling and freeing—work of self-awareness.

It is ego-soothing to blame the other person or

persons for what went wrong, yet blaming will also keep you quite stuck. After all, you hand over a great deal of your power when you blame. You not only make the other person responsible for what ails you, but you give up some say in the solution, leaving him or her to fix it. It is like shackling yourself, because you are then relying fully on someone else to free you from the conflict. It is no wonder that cycles of blame and conflict become so frustrating; they are what my German father would have called *eine Teufelskreis*—a devil's circle—or what in English we know as a vicious circle.

You can break a blaming habit by better understanding the ways you have been snagged and held fast by the conflict.

Conflict and Identity

The first pivot asked you to consider what parts of your conflict have prompted a strong reaction and what you dwell on in your stuck story about the conflict. There is fertile information in those reflections; something important to you is being snagged by the conflict and it is time to figure out what it is. Moore has said, "Look deeply into your fears. Take serious note of your defenses."[8]

Conflict occurs when you perceive that something important to you is being threatened and you decide, even subconsciously, to defend it. In a property dispute, for instance, you may defend the location of your property line. In a workplace dispute, you may defend the way you handled a customer complaint. In a divorce, perhaps you defend your right to live in the house you purchased when you were still a couple.

One common approach to dispute resolution involves helping people negotiate solutions based on their interests. Interests are the underlying needs and reasons for the positions you take in a dispute. In a property dispute, for example, you may care about the amount of land you own because you wish to preserve your investment and maximize property value. In a workplace dispute, you may care about your supervisor's opinion of you because of your desire for job security or opportunity for advancement. In a divorce, you may want to keep your house in order to maintain stability in your children's lives or continue the lifestyle to which you have grown accustomed.

Using interests to resolve conflict is an accepted and common practice, and many thousands of mediators and negotiators use this approach regularly with success. Yet working with everyday interests can sometimes be insufficient. The dispute can get resolved yet the conflict continues—the substantive issue argued over finds resolution, but the friction, strained relationship, or hostility remains and even feeds further disputes. You may have ironed out a divorce agreement, yet find your relationship with your former spouse is badly frayed and a constant source of ongoing frustration. You may have sorted out your workplace dispute, yet find yourself in continued tension with your supervisor. You may have agreed on the location of the property line, yet find yourself constantly vigilant of your neighbor's activities near that line.

If you will never see the other person again, unresolved friction may be of little consequence, except perhaps as fodder for your own self-reflection and learning. If, however, you are in an ongoing relationship because you want to be (you love them, for instance, or they are a close friend) or you need to be (you have no plan to quit your job, for instance, or they are married to your sister), chronic friction presents a problem. Its daily presence is the stuff of distraction, discomfort, even suffering.

What is going on here? The conflict is touching something closer to your core. It is chafing against perhaps your deepest interest of them all: your identity. A divorce may tarnish your self-image as a worthy partner. You may experience your ex-spouse insulting your identity as a good parent. A boss or colleague may challenge your view that you are good at what you do. Your neighbor may inadvertently step on your toes and, in so doing, irritate your sense of independence and clear boundaries. You may find a loved one too smothering for your free spirit, or a friend may hurt you by failing to include you in party plans. Your partner may wound you deeply with a casual remark about your appearance. A war protestor may question your honor; a political rival, your character. Your know-it-all fellow board member may trivialize your expertise.

When something at your core feels threatened or insulted, you experience face loss in one of its many forms, including chagrin, embarrassment, shame, or humiliation. When this happens, it's very difficult to deal with other issues until your self-image feels sufficiently restored; you want the other person to amend the damage they seem to have caused.

Conflict in ongoing relationships is particularly susceptible to what have been called "identity quakes."[9] It's likely that you want your loved ones to see you the way you see yourself. It's reasonable that you want your colleagues to value what you hold most dear about yourself. When you perceive that they don't, conflict has fertile ground in which to take root.

Ongoing relationships can also feed identity-chafing conflict because small insults to your identity can build up over time. In the name of peace, you may choose not to mention the bruised feeling. You swallow and go on, thinking that you're shrugging it off. Then you are figuratively bruised again. And again. There are many places those closest to you can trip up in any given day; you trip, too, of course, inadvertently bruising their identity. It is the human condition. A wall rises one brick at a time.

Sometimes the language someone chooses will alert you to identity-chafing conflict. They will use words and phrases like *disrespect*, *insult*, *criticism*, *disapproval*, *rejection*, *abandonment*, and *character assassination*. Perhaps you have used words and phrases like these.

These words are a type of shorthand that permits someone to avoid discussing the problem at the identity level. Instead of saying, "When you ignored the shipping deadline I set, it suggested to me that you don't take me seriously as your supervisor," you may say, "You need to treat me with more respect." Instead of saying, "When you made that remark about my weight, I reacted strongly because I'm afraid you see me as unattractive," you may say, "Well, have you looked at yourself lately?" Instead of saying, "I'm sensitive about being nagged because I see myself as someone who follows through on my promises," you may say, "Don't be a nag. It's unflattering."

One reason you may avoid discussing the problem at the identity level is that it can feel risky to do so. What if she really doesn't think you're a capable supervisor? What if he really doesn't think you're attractive any longer? What if he really is questioning your integrity?

You may avoid these conversations in the name of self-preservation. Sadly, it is an unfortunate by-product of this avoidance that in the name of self-preservation you may actually prolong and deepen the conflict. You may even end up experiencing more suffering than you would have if you had dealt with the identity-chafing problem directly at the time you first noticed it.

You may also avoid identity-level conversations in the name of relationship preservation. A man said to me about his partner and himself, "I don't want to make things worse by bringing up something so deep. Hell, we can't even handle the easy conversations right now." The unwelcome consequence of this kind of thinking is that, too often, it results in precisely what you are trying to avoid: the ongoing friction damages the relationship, and with enough damage, the long-term result can be divorce, quitting, firing, or other form of relationship disconnect.

Another reason you may avoid addressing an identity quake is that you're not used to connecting the chronic friction you're experiencing with something happening at the core of your being. You may simply be unaware or have gotten used to looking outward for the causes of your discomfort, blaming those around you for what is happening.

Identity-level conversations haven't had the benefit of an easy and commonly understood language for discussing identity threats and insults, perhaps making them feel more convoluted or difficult to raise. I hope the second pivot helps on that front, giving us all a common language for describing and understanding a critical element in the development of conflict.

Yet another reason you may fail to address conflict at the identity level is that you may be too used to arguing over the presenting problem, the problem that presents itself as the apparent cause of a disagreement. For instance, you may find yourself arguing in a committee meeting about whose responsibility it should be to enforce a certain policy. At home you may find yourself arguing about homework or amount of time spent online. Those problems present themselves to you, and you take them on. They suck you in quickly and trap you in their vortex. Yet, as I said in the introduction, if you're in an ongoing state of tension with someone, addressing those presenting problems may well turn out to be Band-Aids at best. When you're in chronic conflict, another presenting problem will be waiting for you tomorrow, wearing down both you and the relationship.

Presenting problems can be very seductive. I am embarrassed to admit that I have more than once argued with my husband about the presenting problem of breadcrumbs on the floor. It's one of those classic, apparently minor skirmishes that couples get into: Should the toothpaste be squeezed from the bottom or the middle? Should it be recapped? Should the toilet seat be lowered after a guy uses it? Should the paper towels unroll over the top or from underneath? Mercifully, we don't skirmish on any of those. I am not that petty. I choose breadcrumbs.

Somehow, my husband butters his toast in such a way that breadcrumbs scatter in a delicate pattern at his feet. I've watched him over the years, trying to figure out why my bread buttering and his yield such different crumb results. Sometimes when I'm standing there watching and beginning to fume, I step outside of myself and am horrified to realize I've probably spent a couple of hours of my life diagnosing bread-buttering problems. I'd like those hours back, please.

I think of it as the Great Breadcrumb Battle. Our

skirmish typically goes something like this:

Me: You're scattering breadcrumbs on the floor again. I just finished vacuuming!

Him: I didn't mean to.

Me: I don't care that you didn't mean to. I care that you did. Intention and impact are two different things.

Him: Please don't do that mediator stuff with me. Anyway, it's just a few crumbs. Gee whiz. Sorry!

Me: It's not about the crumbs, and you know it. It's about me putting in time and effort on something and you disregarding it and devaluing it and messing it up within thirty seconds. There's a whole long list of things like the crumbs. Peanut butter fingerprints come to mind, for example.

Him: Is this going to turn into a long conversation involving martyrdom? Because I'm not really interested. I said I'm sorry. We're done here. [Camera cuts to his back as he walks away with his crumby bread.]

So there we are, arguing about breadcrumbs instead of talking about why I'm so bothered. I'm bothered because there's something else at stake here, something that isn't really about breadcrumbs at all. As foolish as it may sound, those crumbs are causing a minor identity quake.

Six Powerful Conflict Hooks

When the tools and approaches that work in everyday disputes are insufficient or overly complicated, it is time to look deeper. When we want a way to lessen the amount of conflict in our lives, it is time to look deeper. It is time to address the identity-chafing head on. It is time to get clear about our own conflict hooks and how they influence the conflicts we get into, the ways we react, and how stuck we get.

Intercultural conflict and communication theorist Dr. Stella Ting-Toomey has done some particularly enlightening work for understanding identity conflict across cultures. I have found that her ideas are also very applicable to conflict in personal and professional relationships. My students and clients agree; a common sentiment I hear from them after learning about conflict hooks is, "Why am I forty-five and just learning this now? I've needed to know this my whole life."

Ting-Toomey says, "At the heart of many recurring conflict problems often rest unresolved identity conflict needs."[10] She has suggested that there are six broad identity "domains" or types. I choose to call them conflict hooks instead of domains because when something snags them, they hold us in conflict. These are the six broad conflict hooks and the language I use to describe them, adapted slightly from Ting-Toomey's original language:

Competence Hook: Our need to be recognized as capable, intelligent, skilled, or having expertise.

Autonomy Hook: Our need to be acknowledged as independent and self-reliant, and having boundaries.

Fellowship Hook: Our need to be included and to be viewed as likable, cooperative, and worthy.

Status Hook: Our need to be admired for tangible and intangible assets such as attractiveness, reputation, power, and material worth.

Reliability Hook: Our need to be seen as trustworthy,

dependable, and loyal.

Integrity Hook: Our need for others to respect our dignity, honor, virtue, and good character.

The idea is this: when we perceive a threat to a part of our identity we hold dear, we experience conflict with that person. Note the word "perceive." The threat we experience may or may not be real. Mobil station moments arise daily and once we know our hooks, we discover that we can reduce, even eliminate, the skirmishes that turn out to be more about our hair-trigger conflict hooks than about real conflict. Some apparent identity threats turn out to be false alarms. I will say more about this in a bit.

While we may be hooked in any of the categories described above, most of us tend to have one or two hooks that are particularly strong and the most common source of frustration, tension, and conflict for us. As you may have gleaned already from my Mobil station story earlier in the chapter, I have a pronounced competence hook. At even the slightest indication that people think I'm not as bright as they are, as capable as they are, or their intellectual equal, Bad Tammy starts to yawn, stretch, and wipe the sleep from her eyes. I must work to thwart her before she takes control of the reins. Bad Tammy, it turns out, is really Overprotective Tammy.

Once you're aware of conflict hooks, you'll begin noticing the shadow of their presence throughout your day. You'll notice that a testy board member is feeling vulnerable about his place on the board (competence or status hook). You'll notice that your elderly mother, long opposed to selling her home and moving to an assisted living facility, is grappling with the way such a relocation would collide with her view of herself as independent (autonomy hook) and capable of taking care of herself (competence hook). Your ability to see beneath the testiness, beneath the apparent obstinacy, beneath the resistance, will remind you that even when people seem unreasonable, underneath they are usually still reasonable human beings with a normal desire to protect what matters most to them.

Linda, the woman caring for her elderly father, realized she had strong fellowship and reliability hooks. She viewed herself as someone others loved to be around, and she felt particularly isolated now that her father was dependent upon her and she could no longer socialize as she once could. Her brother's lack of participation in their father's care not only resulted in her feeling isolated from work colleagues and friends, but it also felt to her as though he didn't see her as someone he wanted to be around; she experienced this as a direct insult to her sense of self.

Linda also prided herself on being someone others could always count on, and her reliability was well appreciated by employers, friends and family alike. She told me that she's known for being so dependable and loyal that her boss sometimes referred to her as Loyal Linda, a moniker she rather enjoyed. She noticed that her reliability hook was contributing to the conflict because she and her brother both knew she'd be the dutiful daughter and look out for her father even if her brother didn't come through. It made her quite angry to believe her brother was taking advantage of her keen sense of responsibility.

In Linda's case, she didn't just hold reliability as a vital part of her self-identity; she judged others by a high reliability standard and rather often, it turns out, found them wanting. Hers is a good example of the ways we let our hooks get us into trouble not only by being overprotective of our identities, but also by using them to judge and impugn others.

Even less pronounced parts of our identities can occasionally trip us up. Why, in the Great Breadcrumb Battle, did the breadcrumbs bother me so much? It would be reasonable to conclude that I have an interest in a clean and aesthetically pleasing home, and an interest in having my housecleaning effort respected. Those wouldn't be incorrect assumptions. Yet, there are plenty of other people who share those interests and wouldn't have batted an eyelash at my husband's breadcrumb production; they would have simply shrugged it off and gone on with their day. So what was going on for me that made this something I couldn't seem to get past?

Though I didn't recognize it for a long time, perhaps because I wished not to, I did finally notice that I was being snagged by a status hook. Now, I don't think of myself as someone who cares a great deal about material worth, power, and other elements of status, but Ting-Toomey tells us that all six of the domains are part of our identities. So any of them could get tweaked, even though one or two tend to be most pronounced.

The truth is that I do care what other people think about the cleanliness of my home. Perhaps you think that's just ridiculous, and if you do, I suspect you don't have much of a status hook, or your status hook manifests differently. Even I think it's a bit ridiculous. Yet there it is, a status hook that can snag me on occasion. I wish I didn't care. But I do. I've mellowed about it over the years, but it's still there, lurking—and watching for breadcrumbs.

Sometimes, two or more people can both experience

conflict with a specific person, even when their hooks may not be the same. Imagine, for instance, that two managers, Willie and Elise, both dislike one of their colleagues, Nia. Willie experiences Nia's seemingly constant advice-giving, preaching, correcting, and telling him how he should handle things as an insult to his view of himself as a capable manager. Willie has a competence hook and views Nia's unrequested, over-the-top advice giving as implying he isn't measuring up. Elise, on the other hand, does not have a strong competence hook, yet also finds Nia annoying to be around. We discover that Elise has a strong autonomy hook, and her dislike of Nia stems from experiencing the constant advice giving as manipulation and being told how to do her job. Elise and Willy have similar dislike of Nia, yet very different hooks are at the source.

I share this example not just to help you understand more about how hooks influence us, but also because it highlights an error I sometimes see people in groups make when they experience conflict with the same person. The judgment mistake looks like this: A new person joins the department or family, and things get tense. If more than one person in the group doesn't much like the new person, it's tempting to blame the new person for things getting uncomfortable. Original members of the unit see their common negative experience of the new person as confirmation that the problems are the new person's fault.

Now, it is possible, even likely, that the person does have flaws that are contributing to the problems the group is experiencing. It is a failure of the group, however, if its members notice the new person's flaws and stop there in the quest to understand the conflict. It is a failure not to look further, not to understand that in so many conflict situations, there is no single source of responsibility, but a series of small or large contributions made by each person involved. Kottler has made this wise observation: "Every person you fight with has many other people in his life with whom he gets along quite well. You cannot look at a person who seems difficult to you without also looking at yourself."[11]

Delving into the Six Conflict Hooks

Competence

Our competence hooks come from the need to be recognized as capable, intelligent, skilled, or having expertise. Competence is the part of our identity that says to the world, "I am able. I want to be valued for what I'm good at."

Those of us with pronounced competence hooks may find ourselves snagged by real and perceived slights to our talent and intellect. We are more likely to interpret the pursed lips of the Mobil station attendant as judgment about our ability to wave a piece of plastic at a gas pump. We are more likely to worry about how well we measure up at any given task and to defend ourselves heartily when we think another may doubt our ability to be perfect at all times.

A man in one of my audiences said to me after a speech one evening, "I can't help but notice the irony that I doubt my own abilities sometimes but will not tolerate anyone else doubting them." We may hear painful criticism in even the mildest comment or feedback. Our ego is easily bruised if we think someone else doesn't think our smarts or abilities measure up.

Jaclyn, a graduate student in my Interpersonal Conflict class, wrote in her final paper that recognizing her competence hook helped her understand some of her defensive behaviors. She said, "My tendency, when this hook is triggered, is to reexplain my stance, but just with more five-dollar words to validate my point." I loved this comment not only because it showed such good self-awareness but also because Jaclyn's five-dollar words are such an exquisite example of a competence defense.

I have found that when I ask an American audience how many in the room have a strong competence hook, a large percentage of the group will raise their hands. Is it because of our view of our country as an industrious, lift-ourselves-by-our-own-bootstraps kind of nation, born of the hard work and smarts of our forefathers? Is it because we feel the need to prove ourselves as a nation somewhat younger than many others? Is it one way we justify the role our nation sometimes plays in other countries' affairs? Since I work more frequently with American audiences, and in particular business audiences, is my sample just skewed? It is interesting to me that competence hooks seem so prevalent in my American audiences.

Autonomy

Our autonomy hooks come from the need to be acknowledged as independent and self-reliant, and for others to respect our boundaries. Autonomy is the part of our identity that is saying, "I am free. I want you to respect my desire for self-determination."

Those of us with a strong autonomy hook may find ourselves tripped up by situations in which we feel constrained by someone, whether that constraint is real or only perceived. We may take particular issue with being told what to do and may react strongly to someone stepping on our toes. We may hear a suggestion as an attempt to control, and we may too easily hear manipulation in another's words. We may chafe at real and perceived boundaries or rules imposed on us by others.

Once, in a mediation, I had a client who instantly rejected every idea her fellow band member had for resolving the collaboration problems that had arisen. Not even a heartbeat would pass before she'd shake her head and say, "No, that's not going to work." As I watched this behavior and mused, I couldn't help but notice that some of the solutions being offered seemed very much in alignment with this client's clearly expressed wishes. She and I met separately for a few minutes and I shared my observation with her, wondering aloud if I had misunderstood her earlier comments. No, she assured me, I hadn't misunderstood, earlier or now. There were indeed several ideas offered that would work perfectly well for her and resolve some of the problems between them. But under no circumstances was she going to say yes to a single idea of his because that "would feel like obeying his wishes," and she was sick of being his lackey. Now, "obey" was a very interesting word choice and led us to a conversation about autonomy hooks and the role hers were playing in the mediation that day.

Fellowship

Our fellowship hooks come from our need to be included and to be viewed as likable, cooperative, and worthy. Fellowship is the part of our identity that is saying to the world, "I am here! I matter!"

A pronounced fellowship hook can lead us to feel unfairly marginalized or left out, our opinions seemingly undervalued, and our presence unduly excluded from meetings, social events, or other gatherings. These exclusions may cause us to dwell on the situation deeply and in some anguish; we may feel easily bruised by them. Those of us with strong fellowship hooks are highly sensitive to perceptions that someone may not like us or care to be around us.

I once had a client who was experiencing a great deal of ongoing conflict with her former spouse, who worked at the same company she did. This woman was worried that her job was in jeopardy because there were repeated clashes with her ex-husband. As we worked together on the way she was communicating and reacting in disagreements with him, she spoke repeatedly about feeling "dismissed" and "ignored" by him, both now and at the time the marriage ended, and how she would no longer tolerate such behavior from him. This is an example of a pronounced fellowship hook that was badly snagged by what may be the ultimate kind of rejection by a loved one—divorce.

Status

Our status hooks come from our need to be admired for our tangible assets, our intangible assets, or both. Status is another part of our identity that is saying, "I matter. I want you to value my worth."

Those of us with a marked status hook may find ourselves snagged by real and perceived slights to our power or reputation. We may overdefend our image or feel unduly hurt by a casual remark that others may not notice at all. We may take a small criticism as a threat to our reputation. We may fight hard for items of material worth if we believe that their absence from our life will lower our status in the eyes of others whose good opinion we crave. We may go out of our way to surround ourselves with others to convey our importance or power.

I sometimes see status hooks revealed in the way that people fight. Perhaps an employee says, "Everyone feels that way about her; it's not just me," lining up an invisible army of supporters to impart some power and credence to her opinion. Perhaps a mediation client arrives with a large legal team in tow as a display of power, money, and, therefore, status. I once asked an attorney who had not once opened his mouth during a mediation, nor seemed particularly engaged in the event, why he had come. "I'm here for display purposes," he said candidly.

Reliability

Our reliability hooks come from our need to be seen as trustworthy, dependable, and loyal. Reliability is the part of our identity that is saying to the world, "You can count on me. And I want to be able to count on you."

Those of us with reliability hooks are particularly sensitive to real and imagined slights to our allegiance, trueheartedness, and dedication. A casual remark about faithfulness from a partner may launch a storm of anger from us. A supervisor's comment about being a few minutes late for work may set off an over-the-top defense

You will recall that Linda, the caretaker for her father, recognized she had a strong reliability hook. This hook fed the conflict with her brother because not only did her brother not measure up to Linda's reliability standards, but also seemed to be taking advantage of her dependability. It must have felt like treading water far from shore to so want to be viewed as reliable, then have so much responsibility on her shoulders that she feared she wouldn't be able to live up to her own standard.

Integrity

Our integrity hooks come from our need for others to respect our dignity, honor, virtue, and good character. Integrity is the part of our identity that is saying, "I am decent and good. Please respect my good character."

Those of us with pronounced integrity hooks may find ourselves dwelling on embarrassing moments, overthinking and overanalyzing them, replaying them in endless loops in our minds. We may have a hair trigger when it comes to honor, figuratively challenging to a duel anyone who seems to be questioning our good character. We may overdefend our principles and become frustrated when others don't live by the same rules we value.

There is an old story that humorously illustrates the way a hair-trigger integrity hook can run amok sometimes, working too hard to defend our integrity even absent any insult to it:

Fred the farmer needed to plow his fields. But his tractor was in the shop, and the repairs weren't going to be done in time. Fred noticed that his neighbor, Ed, had finished his plowing and decided to ask if he could borrow Ed's tractor.

Fred headed down the lane toward Ed's house, thinking to himself, "I'm sure he won't hesitate to lend it to me. Ed's a good guy and he knows I am, too." A little way further down the lane, Fred mused, "Of course, some folks can be a bit odd about lending expensive equipment." Then he thought to himself, "He'll think immediately about the price of gasoline. I'll need to make sure he knows I'll pay for the gas." A few more steps and Fred realized, "Ed hasn't been over to chat much lately. I hope he's not upset with me about something."

As Ed's house came into view, Fred remembered thinking that Ed had looked at him oddly at the last church supper. "I wonder what that was all about? Did I do something wrong?" he thought. As he stepped onto Ed's front walkway, Fred thought, "I hope he isn't going to make this difficult. I've never done anything to offend him." In his remaining steps to the front door, Fred's mind reeled with all the ways Ed might be judging Fred's good character.

He rapped his knuckles on the door. When Ed answered, Fred said, "You can keep your damn tractor, you selfish SOB. I didn't need it that badly in the first place!" [12]

Of course, our conflict hooks do not live in silos, each separate and distant from the other. Sometimes, conflict hooks overlap. For instance, if you experience your honesty being questioned, you may experience it as a blow to both your integrity (of which honesty is a part) and your status (of which reputation is a part).

A friend once told me that a mutual acquaintance had

remarked about me, "After seeing her speak about conflict resolution at that conference, I expected her to be less opinionated than she is." I understood my friend to be suggesting that I wasn't successfully "walking the talk" in the eyes of this mutual acquaintance. I found myself irritated by the remark, as perhaps my friend wished me to be, and realized that two hooks had snagged me: competence (my ability to "walk the talk") and integrity (my view of myself as authentic and straightforward).

Sources of Our Conflict Hooks

You may well be wondering where your hooks came from and why you have the particularly strong hooks you do. Kottler believes that conflict may represent your attempts to relive dysfunctional patterns that were programmed in your past and that you still use in relating to others. He recommends trying to trace your conflict patterns back to your early years so that you can discover their genesis in your life. Discovering their beginning may well help you neutralize their effect on you, since you may discover that the origins had more to do with someone else's issues and little or nothing to do with you.

Many of my graduate students and clients can recall events and situations that fed their particular hooks (at least as they remember it in that continuously edited videotape we call memory!). Others who cared about the origins found it helpful to discuss their hooks with parents, siblings, and long-term friends, looking for information that offered insights. Still others have found it useful to journal on the matter.

I tried in vain to track my competence hook back to

childhood with my family. I was fortunate to be a winner in the parent lottery, growing up with a mother and father who nurtured, challenged, and supported my abilities without becoming fanatical about it. My father, a German immigrant who came here as a little boy, could not afford to finish high school, dropping out in the tenth grade to help support his family. My mother, the daughter of pragmatic Scottish immigrants, was permitted to attend secretarial school but not permitted to indulge her preference for attending a four-year university, even though her parents had the means to finance a college education. Both my parents believed education to be the key to economic freedom and success in this country and wanted for me what they had not had for themselves. They nurtured my academic competence, though never unduly. I spent plenty of time playing and goofing off, too: building tree forts, swimming, riding my bike with my gang of friends, and riding my horse down long, quiet, country back roads. Many were the times my mother told me to put down *Nancy Drew* and go ride my horse.

I tell you this to convey that, while some hooks may develop from the way a mother or father parented, it is not necessarily the case. The best I could muster after much thought on the subject was to conclude that my particular competence hook blossomed as a result of not wanting to let my parents and teachers down. But who knows?

The question of the source of my hooks is not one that is very compelling to me, I must admit. I don't believe that my failure to definitively track down the likely suspect has prevented me from managing my hooks successfully, nor do I believe that I am somehow avoiding something dark in my childhood. While I highly prize self-awareness and believe it to be the key to better navigating conflict in one's life, it is not in my personality to dig endlessly.

I don't believe it's necessary to know the origins of your hooks in order to manage them or even neutralize their impact on your life. I believe it is sufficient to be intimately aware of them, how they manifest, the early signs you've been hooked, and the most effective ways you can unhook yourself.

You must make your own call on whether or not to pursue an archeological dig for your conflict hooks' roots. For some of you, the pursuit will be compelling and fruitful, perhaps even illuminating. For others, the pursuit will feel less compelling than discovery of the hooks themselves. There is not a single path you must dutifully follow in order to reap the benefits of the conflict pivots.

How Hooks Escalate Conflict

Years ago, I was mediating a conflict between two elderly women who had inherited a large amount of money. Each was represented by an attorney and the attorneys were present in the mediation, along with the women. Increasingly, attorneys mediate in addition to their legal work, and their mediation training and approach often differ in some very important ways from the kind of work I and many other mediators do. Knowing this, I had asked at the beginning of the mediation if either of the attorneys were mediators. Both were. One, the attorney on whom my story centers, told me he had forty hours of mediation training and had mediated several civil cases.

Some time into the mediation, I did or said something that irritated this attorney. I no longer remember what it was, but I do recall the tirade he unleashed in front of everyone in the room. "Who trained you to mediate?" he scoffed. "Do you have even the slightest clue what you're doing?" They were nasty words intended to make me feel small and to make him look like the big man in front of his client.

I experienced his words as an attack on my self-image as a skilled and trustworthy mediator with a reputation for helping people successfully navigate difficult interpersonal conflicts. Immediately, I wanted to defend my skill (competence), trustworthiness (reliability), and reputation (status).

Because his comments were so insulting and made in front of others, I very much wanted to say to him, "You know, when you have forty hours of mediation training it's easy to be unaware of all you don't yet know. But when you've had over 1,500 hours of education and training in conflict resolution, and yourself have trained many hundreds of mediators from all over the world, as I have, you understand that there are multiple different yet still very effective ways to approach a situation like this one." I wanted to defend myself and, as in any good arms race, put him in his place by publicly inflicting on him about the same amount of pain he'd publicly inflicted on me.

If I'd done that, I could have claimed that I'm as fragile a human as the next, which is surely true, but it would have been a blow to the very self-image I wanted so much to defend. Instead, I managed to say (though with shaking hands, as I was still working to control Bad Tammy), "You know, I'm realizing that it might be very helpful to take a moment now and describe some of the ways I work that might be unfamiliar to someone with your mediation training. Let me pause for a moment and do that, and I'll also explain why I'm doing what I'm doing right now." He didn't attack me again, and the mediation continued its course to an agreement several hours later.

By their very nature, our conflict hooks are designed to protect and defend us—to help us save face. Our conflict hooks are a natural part of our personal defense arsenal. And defensive behavior is closely associated with the escalation of conflict. Defensive behavior sometimes creates conflict where there wasn't really any, as in those Mobil station moments I have mentioned before. Defensive behavior can raise the heat level of a conflict as everyone ups the ante in attempts to defend themselves from real, perceived, and anticipated attacks (much like an arms race). And defensive behavior can sidetrack a conflict, causing you to be distracted from the central issues as you travel down a side road to pursue perceived slights and ego-bruising comments.

A man says to me, "He's always dissing me, and I just will not have on my team someone who is so disrespectful." The other man in the room responds in the anticipated way: "I am not treating you with disrespect! Don't I have a right to question anything around here? You are too sensitive." Their conversation becomes a tug-of-war of perspectives: You are disrespectful. No, I'm not. Yes, you are. No, I'm not. They have become sidetracked by a trading of contrasting opinions about respectfulness.

There is no fix for such a conversation except to stop it and do something else to end the tug-of-war. One way that mediators learn to work with feelings of disrespect is to "make it behavioral," that is, to translate the opinion into observable behaviors. So, if a supervisor says, "He is disrespectful," a mediator will often ask the speaker to describe the kinds of behaviors that feel disrespectful. Then, the conversation can focus on the specific behaviors and what to do about them. It is a reasonable approach.

Here's another, more self-directed practice, one to use at the first hints you're feeling disrespected: When you perceive disrespect, turn the mediator's approach on its head and, at least for a moment, make it about you instead of the other person's behavior. Ask yourself, "What part of my identity is being chafed against by the things the other person is saying or doing?" You may find that he or she did not intend disrespect at all but that you just had your own Mobil station moment.

Or, you may conclude it was not a false alarm bell rung by your identity and that you need to discuss the situation with the other person. Then, instead of making the conversation about whether or not that person is disrespectful, you can make it about your experience of his or her behavior. For instance, if you have found your sense of integrity disrespected by a colleague, you can say, "When you questioned the way I handled the customer complaint, it really rubbed me the wrong way. I pride myself on having very good customer service skills and I experienced your question as implying I don't. Is that what you meant to convey?" Who knows where the conversation will go, but one place it won't go is back into the black hole of "Yes, you are" and "No, I'm not."

Another Way Your Hooks Feed Conflict

You'll recall that Linda's reliability hook had another impact: she took what she most highly valued in herself and used it to as a measure of her brother. She said, "I imposed my own high standard of reliability on him, then I judged him for failing to measure up."

Linda's not alone. While my evidence is anecdotal only, I've noticed many clients judging those around them by a standard that's very similar to the part of their identity that they value most. I've seen clients with strong integrity hooks be overcritical of others' integrity and clients with strong status hooks be overcritical of another's economic status or physical appearance.

Perhaps this isn't very surprising. If we so highly value a part of our identity that protecting it can become the stuff of conflict, then it doesn't seem a very big leap to think that the value we place on it extends to the way we appraise those around us. It is probably not coincidence that someone with strong independence and competence hooks, as I have, would marry someone also quite independent and intelligent, as my husband is.

I do notice myself falling into this judging trap, too, and know that it is something I must watch out for. When I judge others harshly, it is often by a competence standard. When I am irritated by someone and my competence hook has been snagged, I will notice myself thinking things like, "Well, he's not very interpersonally adept, is he?" or "Funny that she should judge me when she's not the brightest bulb in the box." It is arrogant, and I must be vigilant about this kind of thinking. You may need to be, too.

False Alarms

For every real and important identity threat, like the one involving the attorney in my earlier story, there are many that don't warrant getting our knickers in a twist.

Our rather sensitive identities get us into trouble sometimes. Knowing our conflict hooks, then, can save us a great deal of trouble and completely erase some conflict from our lives.

I was once asked by a university to assist a small but critically important administrative department experiencing internal tumult. A new director had been hired five months prior and her relationship with her staff had deteriorated to the degree that leadership was inclined to believe they'd made a hiring mistake. Because of the central role this department played in university functions, leadership could not suffer the delays and poor decision-making that this conflict was beginning to cause.

It turned out that the director's primary conflict was with two long-term members of the department. The rest of the staff mostly tried to stay out of it. I focused my attention on the director and the two long-term staff members and, in preparation for the mediation, had several private telephone calls with each of the three. These calls help give me a sense of what's going on and help me prepare mediation participants to bring their best work to the table.

The director told me that the two staff members had never accepted her as their supervisor and had tried to marginalize her from her first day on the job. I asked her what she remembered from that first day that led to such a conclusion. She told me a story about a wonderful first day, with everyone welcoming her, and her delight to be working in that job at that university. She had moved across country to take the new job and was so excited by how pleased the entire staff had told her they were with her hiring.

"Then, at the end of the day, I found out the truth," she said. She overheard one of the two staff members inviting the rest of the crew out for a beer at the local pub. When someone asked if the new director would be coming, the second of the two staff members replied that they weren't inviting her. As she told the story, it was clear she'd played it over in her mind again and again in the months since. Her stuck story was polished and well told.

When I asked what she'd concluded from those events, she said it was very obvious to her that the two staff members had deliberately excluded her, probably because they wanted to go to the pub and talk about her. She said she'd known from that moment that the two of them were going to be a significant problem. And that had proven true.

I inquired if she'd ever asked the staff members about that visit to the pub. No, she hadn't, because she didn't want to give them the satisfaction of knowing their exclusion of her had caused her unhappiness. So, with her permission, I asked them.

Said one, "No, we didn't invite her, though I vaguely remember we talked about whether or not we should." Why didn't they invite her? The second staffer told me, "She had mentioned several times during the day that her condo was almost impossible to get around because of all the moving boxes and how her priority after work for the next week was to get unpacked." Why not just ask her out of courtesy, though, even if they knew she might say no? Said the first, "Because she had been very clear about it several times that day, as though she really wanted us to know her limits. We decided she might view it as ignoring her boundaries if we asked her to come out with us. We thought it would get us off on the wrong foot."

I spoke again with the director, offering the recollections the two staffers gave me permission to share. Her initial response was to push back against their version, to interpret it as a poor attempt to excuse bad behavior. Perhaps it was, yet did she recall feeling overwhelmed by all the moving boxes in her condo? Had she mentioned it to her staff? Was it possible she had mentioned it in such a way that staff could have heard it as a clear message about boundaries? After some consideration, the answer to all these questions was yes.

When we stepped back from the current situation and looked more broadly at conflict in her life, we could see together that a fellowship hook was a significant force in many of the large and small conflicts she'd experienced. She could identify any number of conflict situations, both at work and at home, in which tension arose because she perceived the other person as excluding her in some way, leaving her out of decision making or marginalizing her contribution. She had left her last job because she was frustrated by the presence of an informal "inner circle" her boss had of his most trusted staff members, an inner circle that she could never seem to penetrate.

She realized that when she heard the staff members at this new job discussing the visit to the pub, her fellowship hook filtered what she heard and the meaning she made of it. Whereas I, someone without a strong fellowship hook, might have shrugged it off and stepped around the corner saying, "Can the new kid on the block come to the pub with you all?" this director heard yet another painful instance of exclusion. She built a stuck story around it. And she built five months of interaction with these two staff members around her diagnosis that they were troublemakers who didn't want her as their boss. As too often happens in conflict episodes like this, her treatment of them had become a self-fulfilling prophecy. She had taken a false alarm and made it very real indeed.

It would seem easy to shrug off identity threats that are false alarms. Once you know your conflict hooks, after all, you begin to recognize the false alarms for what they are. The more practiced you are with your conflict hooks, the greater the likelihood that you will master yourself in the moment you're hooked. But if your mood is dark, your stress level high, or your self-awareness temporarily on break, you can still get swept up.

My Mobil station moment is an example of an identity threat that was a false alarm. The threat I perceived wasn't real; it wasn't about me at all. And the perceived threat was so unimportant in my life that it, had I been fully on my game, wouldn't have warranted my attention at all. I wasn't fully on my game that day, though, so I was almost sucked in. Fortunately, I had the wherewithal to check out the threat level before letting loose Bad Tammy on the unsuspecting gas station attendant.

Working with the Pivot 2 Questions

Once upon a time there was a rug merchant who saw that his most beautiful carpet had a large bump in its center. He pressed on the bump with his foot to flatten it out—and succeeded. But the bump reappeared in a new spot not far away. He jumped on the bump and it disappeared—for a moment, until it emerged once more in a new place. Again and again he jumped, scuffing and mangling the rug in his frustration, until finally his assistant lifted one corner of the carpet and a frightened mouse darted out and away.

This story, adapted from one by organizational development authority Peter Senge,[13] illustrates the importance of finding a problem's true source. Like the rug merchant, you may spend too much energy on the bump itself, trying to make it disappear without really understanding it, perhaps causing figurative damage in the process. It is better to follow the assistant's lead, seeking the source.

This is the attitude I invite you to bring to the Pivot 2 questions. Take a deep breath and lift the corner of the rug; look underneath. Don't push the fear or discomfort away. Notice it and embrace it. There is nothing to fear from the mouse beneath the rug; he is you, trying to dodge the pain, trying to get free.

Worksheet Question 4
Why do the things you listed in
Questions 2 and 3 bother you?

Return to your earlier answers and take a careful look at each of them. Why do they bother you? Now, understand, this is not asking you to explain why anyone would be bothered; this is not just another chance for you to look at the bump beneath the rug and say, "Well, no one would like a bump like that!" Strip yourself of the figurative support network behind you. Stand on your own and wonder.

This is a chance for you to figure out what is bothering *you*. Don't jump ahead yet and start naming conflict hooks. Just write out what you find irritating or angering or frustrating or painful about the moments that were the focus of your answers to Pivot 1 questions 2 and 3. You might write things like the following:

- I'm bothered by him implying that my career is

less important than his.

- I'm bothered by the suggestion I'm not a hard worker and valuable employee.
- I was bothered by her implying that we don't have as much money as she does.
- I'm embarrassed that I seemed like an idiot to others in the room.
- I'm bugged that he might think I'm not as fast on my feet as he is.
- I'm irritated that she wants to try to control me.
- I'm bothered that he thinks women aren't—and therefore I am not—good enough to succeed in this field.

Sometimes, people stop too soon in answering this question. For instance, let's consider the way Kara dwelled on her mother's criticisms of her housekeeping, even while Kara worked full-time and was raising two children alone. As we were doing this exercise in class, I asked her why her mother's criticism bothered her so much. Initially she answered, "Because it's unfair." Then, when I waited a bit, she added, "Because my housekeeping isn't her affair."

I invited Kara not to stop there, not to let herself off the hook too soon and before she'd delved deeply enough. I advised her to look for the next "because." I took each of Kara's answers and invited her to pursue that line of thought as follows (my questions in italics):

- *Why does this bother you?* Because it's unfair. *Why do you think it's unfair?* Because it's holding me to a standard I can't possibly keep. *And why does that bother you?* Because it implies I'm a slob.

- *Why does it bother you?* Because my housekeeping isn't her affair. *Why do you care about that?* Because she's sticking her nose in where it doesn't belong. *And why does that bother you?* Because it's yet another way she's trying to control how I live my life.

You can see that her last answers to each query were a great deal more telling, from an identity point of view, than her first.

Worksheet Question 5
What are the ways you see yourself that you suspect the other person may not?

This question is asking you to consider what part of your identity feels put upon by the conflict. Look back at the list of reasons you were bothered. What does that list tell you might have been chafed against during the conflict?

In the housekeeping example from above, Kara realized her irritation with her mother centered on her own identity as a strong, independent woman capable of raising her children well. She heard her mother's criticisms as direct insults about her ability to raise her children in a clean and safe environment and to handle things without having to rely unduly on those around her. Her autonomy and competence hooks had been snagged by her mother's comments.

Not all housekeeping criticisms are about independence and raising children properly, of course. That's what it felt like to Kara, but if your conflict hooks are different, and you have a parent you find critical, the ways your parent's comments chafe against your identity may be different than Kara's. For you it could be status or reliability or even integrity.

Using the bullet point examples from the last section, here are some additional examples of the ways identity can feel chafed by a conflict:

- I suspect he doesn't value my career and earnings.
- I suspect she doesn't see me as a dependable and capable employee.
- I suspect she thinks our business isn't successful.
- I don't like to look like a fool.
- I fear he thinks I'm not as smart as he is.
- I worry she thinks I'm not capable of surviving and thriving on my own.
- I don't like that he thinks I can't succeed in this job.

Worksheet Question 6
What conflict hooks have snagged you in this conflict?

Look at your list of fears and compare them to the list of six conflict hooks. Do you see yourself anywhere in that list of six?

Some people instantly see themselves in one or more of the six common conflict hooks. Indeed, they may have seen themselves somewhere in that list as soon as they read that section. Some hooks are just that pronounced and clear. Perhaps you're in this group.

For others, it may take more reflecting, more peeling back of the layers, like peeling back each layer of an onion. If you're in this group, don't become frustrated with yourself by the lack of an immediate revelation, and don't too quickly dismiss the helpfulness of the conflict hooks idea.

If you're in this group, it can be helpful to look for patterns by considering other conflicts in your life, now or from the past. Complete the worksheet with those conflicts in mind and see what turns up. You may well notice something that was elusive to you when you looked at only a single conflict in your life.

Occasionally, even after reflecting on several memorable conflicts, you may still find yourself unable to classify yourself into one of the six common conflict hooks. That's ok. I don't view it as absolutely necessary that the identity threat you experience fall neatly into one of the named categories in order for you to have success with your conflict pivot. While I've seen that when most people reflect deeply and carefully, one or more of the categories does turn out to apply, I have also worked with a few people who didn't have that experience and who felt strongly that they had conflict hooks that were quite different from the "Big Six."

If you find yourself unable to connect your identity's Achilles' heel with the list here, don't try to needlessly shoehorn yourself in. It is far more important that you begin to discern the parts of your identity you hold most dear, name them what you will, and use them to get yourself unstuck from conflicts that are holding you fast.

5

THE THIRD PIVOT

Pivot Away from the Past and Toward the Now

In 1978, Egypt's President Anwar Sadat and Israel's Prime Minister Menachem Begin signed the Camp David Accords, a treaty brokered by US President Jimmy Carter and for which Sadat and Begin were later awarded the Nobel Peace Prize.

The path to agreement had many potholes. On day thirteen the negotiations at Camp David had completely broken down, and it appeared that Begin and Sadat would return home with no agreement. Carter later related a pivotal moment that kept them at the table:

"Earlier, my secretary, Susan Clough, had brought me some photographs of Begin, Sadat, and me. They had already been signed by President Sadat, and Prime Minister Begin had requested that I autograph them for his grandchildren. Knowing the trouble we were in with the Israelis, Susan suggested that she go and get the actual names of the grandchildren, so that I could personalize each picture. I did this, and walked over to Begin's cabin with them. He was sitting on the front porch, very distraught and nervous because the talks had finally broken down at the last minute.

"I handed him the photographs. He took them and thanked me. Then he happened to look down and saw that his granddaughter's name was on the top one. He spoke it aloud, and then looked at each photograph individually, repeating the name of the grandchild I had written on it. His lips trembled, and tears welled up in his eyes. He told me a little about each child, and especially about the one who seemed to be his favorite. We were both emotional as we talked quietly for a few minutes about grandchildren and about war."[1]

A quarter of a century after the Camp David Accords, I found myself mediating a difficult child guardianship matter. It was a messy family case in which a little girl's grandparents had petitioned the court to be granted permanent guardianship of their granddaughter. The little girl's mother—who was their own daughter—was fighting the petition. At the table were the two grandparents and their attorney, the mother and her attorney, and a court-appointed guardian *ad litem* whose role was to serve the interests of the child. The verbal skirmishes between the three family members began even before they were all seated.

I asked the mother and the grandparents to tell me what was going on between them. The list generated came fast and furious: Her inability to grow up. Their desire to control my life, as usual. Her awful temper and poor anger management. My father can't stand seeing how he's passed down his bad temper to me. He can't stand seeing himself in me! What's right for our granddaughter—being with us. Her vengeful ways. On and on went the list of grievances.

Recalling Carter and Begin at Camp David, I asked if anyone had a photo of the little girl. The grandmother fetched one from her wallet and handed it to me. Staring up at me was an angelic child with blond curls and a white lace dress with yellow bow, her chin resting on her hands, and a sweet smile on the most beautiful little face. It was the kind of photo that would melt anyone's heart. I set the photo in the middle of the table. "Tell me about her," I said.

It was the first real silence in the room. Then together they began to paint a picture of a smart, sweet little girl: A girl who had gotten all As in school that year. A sweet child who ran to her grandfather when he came home each day and curled up on his lap to hear a story. A loving child with a sunny personality despite all that had been going on. A child who doted on her kitty just like her mother had loved her own cat at the same age. A child who was well loved by her mother and her grandparents and who loved them back with gusto.

By now Mom had begun to cry softly. Grandma said softly, looking across at her daughter, "I think she got her love of kitties from you." Mom cried harder. Looking for the first time directly at her father, she said, "She does love being with you, I know that. You are good to her. I know that. But she loves being with me, too, you know." Grandpa nodded almost imperceptibly.

I said to them, "With so much love in the room for this little girl, I wonder what you want to do here today to build on that love and make sure she gets everything she needs and deserves."

Mom dabbed at her eyes with a tissue. "I think we need to make this conversation about what she needs from us all, not about our anger at each other."

Grandpa nodded. "We agree. She needs all of us in her life, somehow." Then he kind of chuckled. "What do you know? That's the first thing we've agreed on in eighteen months."

It's not about photos, of course. It's about staring into the eyes of the present and the future, and then orienting yourself in the same direction. That's the promise of the third pivot.

When the Past Holds You Fast

Siblings who inherited a family business approached me for help. Each made a case for why the other siblings shouldn't have power, shouldn't be trusted, and were damaging the business. They were, of course, playing out a lifetime of wounds not forgotten. Their coalitions changed and morphed, several against one, then several others against a different one. They were playing out decades of frustration with each other, and while they maneuvered and fought, their business was in ever deeper trouble. This had been going on for several years. They were intertwined and stuck like a Chinese wood knot, one of those interlocking puzzles where some pieces hold other pieces fast.

They used the past like a weapon in their conflict. They used it to justify the way they felt and acted. They used it to embarrass and threaten each other. They used it to build alliances. They felt comforted when certain employees took their side, friends in hostile territory, even though the alliances repeatedly proved only temporary. Employees quit or tried to distance themselves from the fray. The siblings were well defended and well stuck, their past-focused habits deeply entrenched. At one level, they were enjoying the fight, even while it was destroying the business their forefathers built from nothing.

We can consider these siblings and intuit quickly that their past was holding them fast. We can see clearly that to unlock the Chinese wood knot of their conflict they needed to turn away from the past long enough to glimpse a possible future.

It is not so hard to see what others must do when held fast by the past. It is often harder to see the same for ourselves, to turn willfully away from what has happened in order to face forward. Some of what holds us back may be a by-product of our stuck story. Some of what holds us back may be our ongoing attempt to figure out it, to keep replaying what happened until we feel like we've got a real handle on it. Some may be the lack of hope that anything can be different and some may be the unconscious choosing of the known over the yet unknown.

There is a Cherokee proverb that says, "Don't let yesterday use up too much of today." The pivots are a way to begin extricating yourself from the grip of your conflict's yesterday. You've already begun that process by the time you reach Pivot 3: your stuck story has been dealt, I hope, a serious credibility blow. You have, I hope, uncovered new insights about the conflict that had eluded you before—knowledge of your hooks—and found a modicum of hope in that new awareness. All of these give you the power to face forward, to help you begin your third pivot.

Taking Serious Note of Your Defenses

Recently, I was caulking around the doors and windows of our newly built garage, preparing for the painters' arrival. I find caulking a tedious task and I'm not very good at it. I usually have as much caulk on my hands as ends up where it belongs. The bead I put down is lumpy and irregular. As I was caulking, my husband sauntered up and suggested he do the remainder of the job. He was very diplomatic about it and made no reference at all to my ineptness.

Perhaps he wasn't thinking about my caulking skill at all and was just trying to help share the workload. Yet in the heartbeat that followed his offer, Bad Tammy opened one eye, wondering whether she should bother to defend me on this one. How ridiculous would that have been? Oh, the horror my life would be if someone else notices I am a bad caulker!

What am I defending myself from in that moment? I am defending against a small insult to my identity as a competent person. Yet the defense is not only unneeded, it is absurd. For when I say to the world, "I am competent!" it is, of course, not fully true. It couldn't possibly be. Though I prefer to be seen as a generally capable human, I am incompetent at many things.

I am an incompetent caulker (alas, now the world knows). I am an incompetent baker; I have all the patience in the world for my clients and none at all for the careful measuring required in baking. I am an incompetent dog groomer, as many clippings of our little dog Luigi (now gone from this world) would attest, one side of his mustache woefully short and little tufts of hair sticking out in odd place all over his body. The list of things I am inept at is long.

This will be true for you, too. If you think of yourself as highly reliable, it is likely that there are circumstances in which you're not fully reliable. If you think of yourself as a person of high integrity, there may be still be a time you tell one friend's secret to another. Even if you're very independent, it's probably true that there are moments you feel needy. And so on. You get the idea.

Taking note of what you're defending yourself *from* helps you determine which path will lead to true freedom from the conflict. If it is a small insult, barely a bruise, then you may take one path. If it is not a bruise at all, but a false alarm, then you may take another. If it is a major identity quake, a bruise of significant scale, yet another path will be required to locate your freedom. I will talk about these paths a bit later in the chapter.

The Problem with Totalizing

One way your conflict hooks keep you stuck in the past is by causing you to "totalize." Totalizing is the experience of viewing something through an all-or-nothing lens. When I'm mediating and coaching, I witness the act of totalizing all the time, in statements like these: He disrespects me. She thinks I'm incompetent at my job. He thinks I'm a bad parent.

When you think and speak like this, it is no wonder that your own version of Bad Tammy begins to gird for battle. You are acting as though your entire identity is being called into question. It is very hard to face forward when you have experienced someone insulting you so significantly.

Yet, it is rarely the case that they were or are. Does he

disrespect every part of your being or does he disrespect the way you acted in the last meeting? Does she think you're incompetent at every part of your job or just the part she raised with you during your performance review? Does he think you're a bad parent all the time or only in certain circumstances? In almost every case, it is the latter, though your conflict hooks cause you to feel as though it's the former. In your attempt to defend the part of your identity you hold dearest, you may totalize what you heard and overreact.

It is much easier to liberate yourself from a conflict hook when you stop totalizing. For instance, while I think of myself as a skilled conflict resolver, I know there are some types of work within the conflict resolution field that aren't a good match for me. Many years ago, I had been hired to facilitate a high-stakes organizational change meeting with a university board of trustees. There was not a lot of difficult conflict, just many implications to consider as they made a decision about the future direction of their institution. Afterward, the president said to me, "Nice job with the facilitation. We got where we needed to get, and you played an important role in that. But I thought you might like to know that you looked pretty bored most of the time, and it rubbed a few people the wrong way."

I was aghast. And ashamed. Because it was true. I had been bored. I had taken the gig because I knew I was a good facilitator and it paid well, but the work didn't feed my soul in the least. When the president said those words, I experienced an identity quake of terrible proportions. I heard my inner narrator say, in a very totalizing way, "You are a pathetic meeting facilitator, Tammy. And he thinks so too!" It didn't matter in that moment that he had also said I had done a good job. My identity as a competent professional had been torn asunder not by the president's comment itself, but by my own totalizing.

In this instance my totalizing response didn't cause me to defend to the death. It caused me to wither and to question whether I should ever take a facilitation job again. Once I had gotten over the shame of hearing those words, I was able to stop totalizing. I was able to hear his words for what they were: A statement that some parts of my work had been excellent and some parts not. It was only then that I was able to figure out what to do with that feedback.

This is your task, too: to stop your conflict hooks from causing you to totalize and overreact to someone's words. Rarely (perhaps never) is anyone truly telling you that you are fully incompetent in life, completely unreliable in everything that you do, or completely without integrity in any way. Your conflict hooks are your Achilles' heels. It is not surprising that someone who prides himself on his competence can easily be hooked by any mention of something he doesn't do well. It's not surprising that someone who prides herself on her independence can easily be hooked by the feeling that someone is co-opting her, telling her what to do, or cramping her style.

Be careful of all-or-nothing thinking, as it will usually steer you wrong during conflict (and in other parts of life, too). Most mediators have learned to view the world in multiple shades of gray. It is not a bad skill to develop in life.

Realizing What You Want for Yourself

Some time ago a casual acquaintance and colleague e-mailed me with a request along these lines: "I'm redoing my website. I was looking at your website and there are turns of phrase that I really like. Is it ok if I use a bit of your language choice here and there on my site?" It was a nice compliment of the work I'd put into my site and I appreciated him asking. I said yes, of course he could.

Months later I visited his website and was startled by what I found. I saw large chunks of language from my own site on his. The design of his site looked visually different, but he had borrowed enough large portions of my language that the sites seemed otherwise rather interchangeable. He had lifted content I had developed over the course of many hours of writing and editing.

I fumed for days. I was irritated with myself for not confirming with him exactly what he meant by "a bit of your language." I was irritated with myself for trusting without asking for more information; clarity about things like this, I know as a mediator, can head off later problems. I was also angry with him. I felt he had taken advantage of my good will and hadn't been fully forthcoming with me about how much he planned to use. My stuck story centered largely on him being a bit slippery, too fast and easy with others' work, and not to be trusted.

I considered what had hooked me. It was easy to see all of his flaws in this situation and more difficult for me to discern why I was so hooked. I kept asking myself, "Why am I caring so much about this?" I realized finally that my autonomy hook was fueling my irritation. I felt he had crossed a boundary and taken advantage of me, classic symptoms of bruised autonomy.

Once I understood what had hooked me, it was time to figure out what to do about it. Initially, my plan was to confront him once I felt less hot under the collar and could handle myself with aplomb. Then I asked myself the question that later became the second question of Pivot 3: What do I most want for myself from here forward?

When I was fuming about the situation, I thought I wanted these things: An apology. Acknowledgement that he overstepped boundaries. Removal from his site of all language he copied from me. Assurance he wouldn't use my content again. But when I pushed myself to consider what I wanted for myself in this situation, my interests turned out to be quite different from the initial list. Once I could see past my bruised autonomy, past the boundary violation, I noticed things earlier blocked from my view.

I noticed that I wanted my website to be unique and reflect who I am and how I work. It might seem that the easiest way to achieve what I wanted was to make sure the copycat removed the borrowed content. But then I realized something very important to me: if my friend saw himself so easily in my words, then I had not done a particularly good job of distinguishing myself from others. After all, he and I were quite different experientially, stylistically, and even in the kind of conflict resolution work we did.

I noticed that I really wanted to spend minimal energy on something that probably would not turn out to matter a whole lot in my life. I found myself wondering whether confronting him would turn out to be as clean and tidy a task as I'd initially assumed. Maybe it would be. But maybe it would get complicated, and then I'd find myself putting energy into it. I finished this line of thought with the conclusion that confronting would probably be fairly straightforward but did carry a small risk of becoming time-consuming.

I was surprised to realize that confronting my friend

would not help me make much headway toward what I really wanted. To achieve the results I most wanted for myself in this situation, I made two decisions: I would not confront him and I would rework the language on my own site.

Conflict hooks can distract you from realizing what you really want for yourself in the conflict, as mine almost did. One way they distract is by causing you to pay so much attention to the perceived insult that you pay too little attention to other needs you have in the conflict, some of which may be equally or even more important. Another way they distract is by causing you to put so much effort into restoring face that you only consider solutions that achieve that goal, missing other viable options. One purpose of Pivot 3 is to help you see past the distractions in the same way it helped me see past the alarm raised by my autonomy hook.

I know you may be surprised by the decisions I made in the website situation, perhaps even consider them ill-advised. I was surprised myself. I have told the website story to my graduate students, using it as a classroom exercise in clarity and decision making in conflict situations. They invariably say to me, as you may also be thinking: Wait. How can you let him get away with that? Doesn't it leave a bad taste in your mouth that he took advantage of your work? Isn't it a mistake to leave him thinking he did nothing wrong? Won't you be allowing him to do something similar to others? Are you sure you're not just being an avoider?

Now, those who know me well know that I am very far from an avoider. Most would say, in fact, that I should learn to avoid more. So I ask my students in return: Why do you believe it should become my job, and take my time, to educate him? Why do you believe that if I tried to persuade him he overstepped professional boundaries that he would fundamentally change? Why do you diagnose me as an avoider without knowing me well enough to make that call? Why do you believe that in the grand scheme of my life, taking time on this fellow, a casual acquaintance who is not an important friend in my life, is worth trading away time from something else I might value more? On what basis have you determined that the choice you would make for me is a better one than the one I chose?

You see, sometimes people around you will not understand or agree with what you want for yourself. They may have their own list of rules and "shoulds" they want you to adopt. They may have their own agendas. They may care so much about you that they also get swept up in protecting your identity. This all further complicates reaching the kind of clarity you need to achieve your freedom from the conflict, of course. It is part of what makes conflict get more complicated.

You must try to avoid getting swept up in what others want for you. I am not saying you should ignore them entirely and assume they have nothing helpful to contribute to your thinking. Indeed, hear them out. But do differentiate hearing them out from the need to adopt their views of your world.

Letting Go When It's Real but Not True

I said in the introduction that the conflict pivots would help you down one of two paths in your conflict: let it go and move on or determine precisely what you must discuss with the other person so that something shifts in your conflict. You are at the stage now with your pivots that it is time to scrutinize the paths open to you and discern which will serve your freedom best.

Sometimes, by the time you get to Pivot 3, you already know you can let go of what hooked you because you now recognize it as real but not true. You've glimpsed your conflict hooks, perhaps even grown quite familiar with them by the time you read this, and you see that the conflict wasn't really conflict at all; it was just your own hooks snagging you or your own residual fear enveloping you.

Letting go because it's real but not true is the right choice when you are experiencing your own Mobil station moments, the trivial false alarms in an average day. It is also the right choice when you recognize that your spouse's attempts to push your buttons aren't that at all, but simply them being themselves and your hypervigilant conflict hook sounding the alarm. Or when you notice your conflict hook's sensitivity is causing you to overreact to a fellow board member's reasonable questions about your proposal. Make this your mantra for letting go in such moments, much like Tsoknyi Rinpoche made it his: *real but not true.*

Occasionally, you won't be sure right away if it's real but not true. This is a good time for you to lead with your curiosity. You can ask, as I did with the Mobil station attendant, "What do you mean?" You can ask this in other ways: "What are you trying to say?" "Can you say more about that?" You will have to check out the perceived threat, and it is a good use of your energy to do it. After all, if you don't, it could take a great deal more of your energy navigating a conflict that you alone initiated.

In every argument, there's a moment when you choose to fight. It may not seem a choice, because the moment is fleeting and the decision is often not a conscious one. But choose you still do. I call such moments "choice points," the points at which you can choose one path or another. With awareness, you can begin to notice these choice points and make thoughtful choices about how to proceed. Your goal is to notice the choice point before you are swept up in the current of conflict, particularly those that are real but not true.

Knowing that such trivial conflicts are ones to let go does not mean that you will automatically find it easy to do at first. You may have to practice consciously releasing the perceived threat until the practice has its own well-worn path in your heart and mind. Over time, if you're like me, you will find the unhooking becomes easier, even rapid, in such moments, and you will inwardly smile and shake your head at how such things used to snag and hold you.

Years ago I created a brief visualization to help me let go of things that nagged at me but weren't important. Perhaps you will find it helpful as well. This visualization works best if you can find a quiet spot for a couple of minutes, someplace where you won't be interrupted or disturbed and where you can close your eyes.

Picture this in your mind's eye: It's a sunny, beautiful day, just the perfect temperature. You're walking on a gravel path with the warmth of the sun on your face, a light breeze moving across your cheek. You hear the birds chirping. You smell the fragrance of spring flowers. All your senses are alive.

You reach a low footbridge extending over a small creek. You walk up on the footbridge, which curves upward to an apex. Picture the sound your footsteps make on the wooden bridge, the feel of your body moving up a slight hill to the point where the bridge is the highest, just a few feet above the water. You stand near the waist-high railing at the apex and gaze downstream, watching the water move and curl and recede into the distance. Hear the birds chirping and feel the breeze again.

Cup your hands as though you're about to receive a gift in them. But today you're not receiving; you're giving. In your cupped hands is the memory, the trouble, the problem, the thing you want to let go of. Look down and see it there. You say good-bye to it, not with venom or sadness, just with clarity. Good-bye.

You toss it from your cupped hands into the water below. It lands with a slight splash and begins to move away from you in the current. It bumps for a moment against a submerged rock, and then continues downstream. You never take your eyes off of it. You watch it until it reaches the point where the creek's water also disappears from your sight. Good-bye for good, you say.

You raise up your arms and stretch slowly, luxuriatingly, feeling what it's like to have a weight off your shoulders. Then you turn, not looking again at the water, and continue off the far side of bridge, into your future.

Letting Go for Freedom's Sake

On February 11, 1990, then-Arkansas governor, Bill Clinton, sat with his daughter, Chelsea, and watched on television as Nelson Mandela exited a South African prison. Clinton wondered what Mandela was thinking as he took the long walk toward the prison gates, a walk to freedom that was twenty-seven years in the making. Some years later, Clinton had a chance to ask Mandela about that moment. He said, "I know you are a great man. You invited your jailers to your inauguration. You put your persecutors in the government. But tell me the truth. Weren't you really angry all over again?"

Mandela replied, "Yes, I was angry. And I was a little afraid. After all, I'd not been free in so long. But when I felt that anger well up inside of me, I realized that if I hated them after I got outside that gate then they would still have me." Then he smiled and said, "I wanted to be free so I let it go."[2]

This is a more difficult type of letting go, but you do not need to be a Nelson Mandela to achieve it. In such instances, your conflict is real *and* true, and your desire to confront may be fully justified. Perhaps you feel confident that confronting the conflict head on will yield results that are satisfying to you. Others may be watching your conflict unfold, or have opinions about what you should do; these can feel like added pressure on you.

Sometimes, the trade-off of your emotional energy, your time, even your resources, does not make it worth it to you. You decide you want your liberty from it more than you want to search for an agreed-upon resolution. You decide that you can preserve or save face from the identity insult without them having to change their thinking or actions, as I did with the website situation discussed earlier. Poet and philosopher Mark Nepo has said that pain is necessary to know the truth, but you don't have to keep the pain alive to keep the truth alive.[3] You can keep the truth about yourself—your value to the world and to those around you—alive without allowing the discomfort and pain to rule you.

If you are ready to let go in circumstances like this,

you must do so fully and with real commitment. This means that you are letting go not just for now, but for good. Letting go is not about packing it away until the other person does something you don't like, then pulling the old conflict out of the steamer trunk, dusting it off, and using it to fuel your self-righteousness and indignation. Pulling it back out of the trunk later isn't letting it go; it's postponing. Things tend to fester while you postpone indefinitely, so this is not a very good strategy for resolving conflict.

Keep in mind that letting go for the sake of your freedom is not the same as severing the relationship. There are times, certainly, when you may not value a relationship enough that you want to nurture it, but that is not what I am talking about here. I am saying that there are times, even in very important business and personal relationships, where you weigh the pursuit of a conflict against letting it go and moving on, and decide the latter is your best choice. You decide that, in the grand scheme of your life with this person or in the grand scheme of your business relationship with this person, this will not matter.

Sometime after Clinton and Mandela discussed Mandela's departure from the prison on Robben Island, Clinton found himself in the midst of one of his own difficulties. Mandela sent a message to Clinton via Thabo Mbeki, South Africa's president at the time: "Mandela said I should remind you to let it go."

When Old Habits of Mind Thwart You

Sometimes you are very sure you want to let it go and you have done the self-work to make sure it's the right call. You feel committed to your decision. Then the other person walks into the room or does something, and you find yourself transported back to where you were before you began pivoting. You find yourself feeling irritated and swept up again.

My yoga teacher, Balmeet, is fond of saying, "Discomfort is your friend but there are no points for pain." Discomfort signals something you may wish to work on, while pain is a warning that real injury is imminent. So, if you stumble while making a committed effort to move past a conflict that has plagued you, recognize the stumble as another ally, an ally reminding you to continue practicing the commitment to let go. There is no need to chastise yourself harshly and turn your misstep into pain.

Remember, if the conflict has plagued you enough, then your stuck story and the state of tension in the conflict may well be long-term habits. Perhaps you are also strongly reactive to one of your conflict hooks, and this is also a long-term habit. So, even if you know intellectually that it is the right choice to move on, there can still be a gap between what you know and what you tend to do. These are moments that can test your commitment to let go.

If you decide to let go for the sake of your freedom and, sometime later, discover that you did not really do so and it is more than just old habit, then there is something you have not yet fully addressed. I find it helpful to revisit the Pivot 3 questions on those occasions.

Talking It Out: Explaining Yourself

Sometimes, Pivot 3 doesn't result in a decision to let

it go. You take a close look at what you most want for yourself in the situation and decide that you can't fully achieve it without a conversation. There are many good reasons to talk further about the conflict with the other person.

Perhaps you wish to make the other person aware of the reasons for your reaction and demonstrate that you're working on your hair-trigger hooks. Jon, a client of mine a few years ago, was in a rough patch with one of his own clients after losing his temper. He had blown up in a grandiose way and was concerned not only about losing the client, but also that the client would lodge a complaint with one of his profession's oversight boards. He wanted to be able to demonstrate to this client that he was getting a handle on what had caused his verbal explosion and to convince him that he didn't have to worry about it happening again.

As Jon and I worked through his conflict hooks, the message he needed to convey to his client became ever clearer. He decided on an approach along these lines: "I didn't just surprise you with my anger—I surprised myself. I was shocked and determined to figure out what caused me to overreact and damage a professional relationship I value. After a lot of soul-searching, I realized that when you questioned some of my data, I took it as a direct insult to my competence and integrity. When I view your questions calmly now, I see you were attempting to understand the data and make sure we were on the same page in how we interpreted it. I wish I had realized that then. What happened gave me new insight about myself that will help me avoid blowups in the future. I've got some work to do, and I will do it. I hope you will allow me to continue to serve as your consultant on this project."

The point of this kind of conversation is not to defend, deflect, or explain away your reaction to whatever happened. It is a conversation intended to demonstrate your self-awareness and help the other person understand why things unfolded the way they did for you. One of my students, Taryn, said in class, "Now I can say, 'Let me tell you about my conflict hook and why what happened had such an impact on me.'" This is such a lovely way to broach this kind of conversation because it is simple, clear, and without defensiveness.

Talking It Out: Recalibration Conversations

Perhaps you need to talk with the other person about the ways the conflict is chafing against both of you and causing repeated unrest in the relationship. These can be some of the most important conversations of our lives because they help recalibrate our relationships, consciously adjusting how we engage each other.

Recalibration conversations are not problem-solving conversations. Their purpose is not to take a specific dispute and negotiate a mutually agreeable solution. Recalibration conversations are conversations anchored in identity: how you see yourselves, how you perceive the other is viewing you, how to handle identity quakes when they come up, how to help each other notice when one of you has been snagged. They are a very special kind of heart-to-heart and they have one goal: to begin easing a strained relationship by talking about a topic that often flies below the radar in relationships.

Recently, I chatted with Eva, who found herself in conflict with her husband over the future of their family farm. Her husband had inherited the farm from his father and was the fifth generation to operate the farm. She and her husband had run the farm for thirty-five years and were beginning to discuss their retirement and what would become of the farm.

They were at deep odds about it and there had been any number of very nasty exchanges between them, many ending with either Eva or her husband storming out the door. Eva had attended one of my workshops and approached me afterward to seek out additional advice. She told me she realized during the workshop that the conflict was chafing against her fellowship hook because her husband seemed to be disregarding her as his partner on the farm. He had even once said that she'd "just married into" the farm and wasn't vested in it the way he was. He had said this when he was very angry, as will happen.

Eva guessed that her husband had a strong autonomy hook, and this insight gave her a new way of understanding the conflict dance they were in. She danced ever closer to her husband, wishing him to acknowledge all she'd done for the farm over many years and the value of her opinions. She danced so close, in fact, that perhaps she stepped on her independent husband's toes, causing him to pull away from her. On they danced, him pulling away as an assertion of his autonomy and she stepping closer as an assertion of her desired fellowship.

I recommended to Eva that she and her husband temporarily suspend the conversation about retirement and focus first on exploring how the farm conflict was chafing against them and straining their relationship. They may have been able to push their way through the tension to reach a retirement decision, but I suspect that they would have a great deal more strain in the relationship before they were done.

I suggested that Eva might invite her husband into this kind of conversation by broaching it along these lines: "When we discuss what to do with the farm and we get angry, sometimes you say things that I experience as dismissive. When that happens, my insides just quake because I think of myself as someone who has helped this farm survive. I imagine I also say things in those moments that make you quake, too. I learned something in a workshop today that I think might help us understand why we both get so angry about this, and I'd really like to talk about it with you."

Linda, whom we've followed throughout the book, decided she wanted a conversation like this with her brother. Her work in Pivot 2 helped her see how the situation was hooking her and why her prior conversations with her brother yielded such poor results. She wanted both to acknowledge her own role in the conflict and to see if they could address together the way the conflict was chafing against her identity—and perhaps his as well.

Linda had identified the following as the things she most wanted for herself going forward:

- Enjoy more of the time she spends with her father and make his final days as happy as possible
- Carve out rest and relaxation time for herself
- Not feel bitter about the weight on her shoulders
- Have a strong relationship again with her brother

Linda was quite energized by what she'd learned from pivoting and was ready to bring this list to her brother. I was concerned that if she did, the conversation could

spiral into its old habits, with her sharing yet another list
of wants with a brother who would not or could not
deliver them. So I pushed Linda to do something else
first, something that would require her to dig deeper
before talking to her brother. I wanted her to look at her
list and pretend that her brother was not available to
figure things out with her. What would she herself do to
bring her own interests to fruition?

Because she was used to expecting an external
source—her brother—to help her achieve what she
wanted, Linda was challenged by this question at first. I
encouraged her to ponder it for a few days and see what
came up; I wanted her to push herself and not too easily
give up and assume her only relief came via her brother.

To enjoy more of the time she spent with her father
and make his final days as happy as possible, Linda
decided to keep reminding herself that her father's
remaining days were limited. She had been so swept up by
feeling abandoned and taken advantage of by her brother
that she had allowed bitterness about it to darken
interactions with her father. When she considered how
she'd feel the day after her father passed away, she
realized she would feel relief—and something more: she'd
feel immense sadness and a hole in her life. Linda decided
to keep this reminder present in her mind and to do
things with her father that gave them both joy, like
watching funny movies. She'd long wanted to interview
her father about his life and create a DVD for her
cousins, and she decided to stop putting it off.

To carve out rest and relaxation time for herself,
Linda decided to set aside a few hours each week as "me"
time and to hold that time sacred. She realized she
had made herself available to her father 24/7 and that
they had both gotten used to thinking of her as always

"on duty." She felt certain her father would not begrudge her time to herself and would be happy to honor her down time. In a very candid moment Linda said, "I've been making myself a reliability and fellowship martyr, overplaying the burden and loneliness in an attempt to make my brother see my unhappiness."

Linda also decided she needed to do something about her isolation from friends, which had happened gradually as she spent more time caring for her father and had taken a leave of absence from work. Her identity had suffered from these withdrawals from social and work life, as she had previously enjoyed fellowship with friends and the appreciation she experienced for being someone everyone liked.

To begin rebuilding a strong relationship with her brother, Linda decided that she needed to spend more of their conversations talking about his life and just enjoying being with him from afar. The conflict had become so all-encompassing that every phone conversation focused on it, and they had both stopped talking about other things important in their lives.

When she challenged herself to really consider what she could control all on her own, Linda found that she had the power to bring many of her most important interests to fruition by herself. Some of them were even *better* brought to fruition through her own actions than through any action of her brother. She not only realized she could achieve her goals without relying on her brother's contribution, but she also realized that she could bring them to fruition without spite. In other words, she could act without doing it in a way that fed her anger or spite toward her brother.

Instead of feeling burdened and abandoned by her brother, Linda was now feeling strong and at greater peace about her circumstances. She said, "Before, my conversations with my brother came from a place of anger and neediness. Now, I'll be coming from a place of calm strength. While it would be nice if he helped in some way with our father's care, I no longer *require* him to." Linda had gone a long way toward unhooking herself from the conflict all on her own.

We returned to the conversation she wanted to have with her brother. Linda had several questions she wanted to ask him: What can I do to help keep our relationship healthy during this difficult time? What will you do? Are there things you've wanted for Dad but that our conflict has prevented you from doing? These questions were ones that had not occurred to Linda before the three pivots. She had been so clear that her brother was the one who was flawed and needed to change that she had not been willing to consider ways he might be wishing she, too, might change.

Linda's conversation with her brother would be very different than the ones they'd had so far. She had clarity about what was most important to discuss, and so their conversation would be focused and potent. She understood that the conversation would not lead suddenly to a perfect resolution and that the tension would not miraculously disappear. But she had taken her power back and figured out how to find peace of mind through her own thoughts, choices, and actions.

Recalibration conversations have the greatest likelihood of success in situations where each person in the conversations wants (or hopes) to stay in the relationship, such as situations between a married couple, people living together, business partners, siblings, best friends, and, in the right circumstances, between supervisor and direct report. I say "in the right circumstances," meaning that recalibration conversations are, by their very nature, intimate, and not every workplace or supervisory relationship will lend itself well to recalibrating in this way.

Is it possible to have a successful recalibration conversation with, say, your ex-spouse, whom you see regularly because of your children? If both of you want to have this kind of conversation, it can be very successful and very powerful indeed for dissolving chronic tension and conflict. If only one of you wishes to have this conversation, however, I suspect that you will find it frustrating and draining. You are better served by using Pivot 3 to figure out what you most want for yourself from here forward and how you will achieve it by your own thoughts and actions.

Working with the Pivot 3 Questions

Sometimes the new clarity gained from Pivot 2 gives you such relief that you are tempted to skip the third pivot or to gloss over the Pivot 3 questions. I encourage you not to do either.

Psychologist Jeffrey Kottler, whose thoughts I have shared in other parts of this book, has noticed that students of psychology, people who have been in therapy for years, and those who can easily hold forth on numerous psychological theories with some frequency still find themselves "enlightened wrecks." You see, understanding past mistakes doesn't automatically lead you to not repeat them. In Kottler's own words, legitimate learning takes place only when you put your insights to work, when you take responsibility for your predicament.[4]

Pivot 3 is very specifically designed to help you put your insights to work, to translate them into substance. It is designed to prevent you from stopping just short of your true freedom.

Worksheet Question 7
What are you protecting yourself from?

This question is asking you to take serious note of your defenses, to take down your shield and set your verbal weapons aside. Consider how you have been hooked by the conflict. What are you defending? Do you need such a strong defense? Is it both real and true?

You may discover that you are protecting yourself from a minor insult to your identity, similar to a Mobil station moment. In such instances, the third pivot is likely complete for you now, because there's nothing about the situation that you need to attend to. You're done and moving on.

You may discover that the thing you are defending yourself from is so distressing that you have been doing almost anything to avoid acknowledging it. If you have been your supervisor's right-hand man and a new colleague threatens to supplant you in that role, you may undermine that new colleague to the boss at every opportunity. I have seen this done. If you fear that your fiancé is having doubts, you may start many small fights to test his love. I have seen this done.

Perhaps your business partner makes an investment decision without you and your fellowship hook is snagged. Instead of raising the specter of being marginalized, you choose to talk about his apparent underhandedness. Perhaps your husband tells you his opinion matters more in deciding what to do about the farm because it's really more his farm than yours. Your identity as a beloved spouse and contributor to the farm's success has a major quake, but instead of discussing these, you try to convince him to listen to your advice about the farm.

I said earlier that taking note of what you're defending yourself from helps you determine which path will lead to true freedom from the conflict. You must be clear about the "threat level" to know how much more energy to put into it.

Worksheet Question 8
What do you want for yourself from here forward in this situation?

This question is asking you to turn your focus deliberately away from what's happened and toward the present. I am asking you: How do you want to feel and be? What will give you peace of mind and freedom from your stuck story and the way you've been hooked? How will you restore face if you experienced a face loss?

At first, a couple comes to me unhappy with their relationship, which is filled with recrimination and a litany of past transgressions on both sides. They can only talk about how miserable the other person is making them and their doubt that the relationship should continue. They cannot stop looking at the pain and misery in their wake. Later, their Stuck Stories exposed for what they are, they are able to paint a picture of the future they each want. One talks about wanting to come home from a long day at work happy to be home and with someone she loves. One talks of waking up on weekend mornings looking forward to the day ahead instead of experiencing a feeling of dread in anticipation of two back-to-back days of tension. They discuss the way they have each become overreliant on the other for determining their own happiness, and they imagine what they each might do on their own to build individual happiness and, in the process, become happier together. This is what it means to know what you want for yourself from here forward.

Before learning how to pivot, Linda had a very clear sense of what she wanted, and she'd even hired me to help her get it: she wanted to persuade her brother to play a much larger role in the care of their father. What she wanted for herself was to carry less of the load and ease her stress. After learning how to pivot, you'll recall that Linda identified her wants differently. She said, "I want to enjoy more of the time I spend with Dad. I want to make his final days as happy as I can. I want not to be bitter. I want more freedom in my day and to have a social life again. I want to have a sound relationship with my brother, since he'll be the only immediate family I have left after my dad passes."

What do you notice about those two sets of desires when they are contrasted with each other? I notice that the first is a desire that can be brought to fruition only through external means (her brother changing his ways); the second set of desires is largely within her own power. The first relies on how canny a negotiator she can be with her brother; the second relies on decisions she will make for herself. Fixing her brother largely motivated the first; addressing important identity needs motivated the second. The first list is about her easing her suffering; the second is about happiness and freedom. Which kind of list do you want?

Worksheet Question 9
What will you do to make this possible
for yourself?

This question is asking you to stop relying on what the other person will or won't do and to consider what you yourself have the power to do. How will you command your own future? What will you do to address this conflict that has sidetracked you? How will you use your knowledge of your hooks to reduce conflict in your life?

To answer Question 9 well, you need to have answered Question 8 well. You must look at the things you most want for yourself in the current situation and use Question 9 to figure out how to reach those things on your own, without relying on the other person. For who knows if he or she will ever do what you want?

Sometimes, you will choose to let the conflict go because it was a false alarm. Or maybe you've decided that letting go helps you reach your true goals or that letting go enables you to choose your freedom immediately. Maybe you have decided that your best effort is placed in becoming more acquainted with your conflict hooks so that you can more easily keep your balance during identity quakes.

Sometimes, you will choose to talk things out with the other person, finally able to orient yourself toward what the conflict or the tension has really been about for you. You now know precisely what you should discuss with the other person so that real resolution between you is within your grasp. It must be a conversation anchored in the self-knowledge of your conflict hooks and in your keen awareness of what you most want for yourself going forward. These are the things you must discuss; these are the "right" problems to focus on when you confront the conflict head on.

If you choose to talk things out, be aware of your goals for the conversation. Goals like these will get you trapped, as they have trapped you all along: "Get him to [fill in the blank with whatever you want him to do or not do]." "Make her understand." "Persuade him to see it my way." These goals are still about the other person and what he or she must do or not do. If you choose goals like this, you are giving away your power again because you have no real ability to make the other person do anything.

If you choose to talk things out, goals like these can have a powerful and positive impact on your conversation: "Explain what hooked me and explore ways to address it." "Explore ways the conflict has hooked us both and what to do about that." "Begin easing a strained relationship." "Figure out how to reconnect." Goals like these are the essence of recalibration conversations, those relationship-altering foundations on which you build your present and future.

When Talking It Out Doesn't "Work"

Many years ago the professor to whom I reported for my graduate teaching fellowship handed me some textbooks and told me that the classes I was TA'ing (serving as a teaching assistant and, in this case, teaching largely on my own) would start the following week. My graduate studies were in higher education, and by some strange roll of the university administration dice, I ended up reporting to an elementary education professor. I said to him, "But I don't know anything about elementary education!" To which he replied drily, "Well, then, stay a chapter ahead of them." It is the way, unfortunately, that far too many graduate students and future college professors first learn to teach—by staying a chapter ahead.

The night before my twenty-three-year-old self had to teach my first college class—my first class of any kind, anywhere—I was in a state of near panic. I called a friend and said, "I don't know what I'm doing! I don't know what I'm talking about! I don't know anything about elementary school children. I was never even a babysitter! They're going to see me for the fraud I really am. I don't even know if I've got enough material for a one-hour class!" After she'd talked me off the ledge, she said, "Have some spare material in case you run out."

That's when I began developing what I call "back pocket material," the exercises and ideas I can keep figuratively tucked in my back pocket in case there's spare time in a workshop or class and I need additional content. I rarely draw on it, but I'm always comforted to know it's there.

Remember how, earlier in this chapter, I described pushing Linda to pretend that her brother was not available to figure things out with her? Games of pretend like this can be extraordinarily helpful because they give you permission to explore a possibility without any commitment at all. You don't have to worry whether or not you'd ever consider the possibility seriously; you are just playing around with an idea. I pushed Linda to figure out, before she spoke to her brother, what she herself would do to bring her own real goals to fruition in the event that she and her brother could not resolve matters together.

This is not a new idea, but it is an idea that is primarily discussed in negotiation training. When you walk into a negotiation knowing you've got a terrific alternative if the negotiation doesn't bear fruit (in the jargon of the field, BATNA, or your Best Alternative To a Negotiated Agreement), you will be less desperate, less on edge, less reliant on what the other person will agree to at that moment in time. This will ground you.

I encourage you to push yourself in the same way I pushed Linda before you talk things out in your personal and professional relationships. Figure out how you will bring your own wants to fruition whenever possible. When you do, you'll have your very own back pocket material.

PART 3
THE HABIT

6

QUESTIONS AND ANSWERS

The following are some of the most frequently asked questions about pivots and pivoting. To submit your own question and see questions other readers have asked since the book went to print, visit the book's website listed in appendix A.

1. Are three pivots really all we need?
2. Are you saying that all conflict is caused by perceived insults to our identities?
3. Are you saying the conflict is my fault?
4. What if someone is trying to press my buttons?
5. Are you saying that inner work is the answer to all my conflict problems?
6. But I know my stuck story is right.
7. But everyone agrees with me about the other person.
8. How can I unhook myself when the identity insult really is true?
9. What if the other person really doesn't see me the way I see myself?

10. Do the pivots allow us to let ourselves off the hook too easily?
11. Aren't the conflict pivots just a fancy form of avoidance?
12. Isn't this just about putting spit and polish on a bad situation?
13. Why didn't my pivots "stick"?
14. What about dealing with difficult people?
15. Is this like cognitive behavior therapy?
16. Can I use the pivots in conflicts that involve more than one other person?
17. How big a conflict can make use of the pivots?

Please visit the website referenced in appendix A for additional questions that have come in from readers.

1

Are three pivots really all we need?

One of the guiding principles behind the development of the pivots was "Complicated stuff doesn't need more complication." I wanted to identify a few straightforward, simple practices that would move you a very long way toward truly resolving interpersonal conflict.

Three pivots seem like the right number to me because most of us can remember three things, even in the midst of high-heat moments. And, practiced together, the three pivots result in tremendous changes and progress.

When you find yourself lost "in the weeds" of a conflict, try backing out and returning to a few simple ideas.

2

Are you saying that all interpersonal and relationship conflict is caused by perceived insults to our identities?

I believe that interpersonal conflict is born in the tangled interplay of identity, vulnerability, and perception.

We hold our identities dear, as they represent who we are and how we want to be valued by others. The shadow side of our firm grip on identity is vulnerability, the fear that others will not view us in the way we wish or the fear that we are not fully who we wish to be. When we perceive a threat to our identity (whether or not the threat is real), we feel vulnerable and are tempted to defend ourselves against the threat. This is the moment that conflict can be born.

This is a book about dealing with conflict in ongoing relationships and avoiding the false alarms. In my experience, these kinds of conflict can often track their source back to identity.

3

Are you saying the conflict is my fault?

No. Maybe. Yes.

No: States of tension and conflict between people in ongoing personal and professional relationships are often the result of walls being built one brick at a time over a long period. You're doing things that are contributing to the conflict. The other person is doing things that are contributing to the conflict. Together, you dance.

Maybe: Michael, a participant in one of my seminars for a New York hospital, told this story: A man gets on the elevator with his dog. At the next floor, a second man gets on the elevator, scowls, and says angrily, "Why is that dog on this elevator?" The dog growls at the man. On another floor, a third man gets on the elevator. He smiles at the dog and says, "You are such a cute fellow!" The dog wags his tail happily at the man. So where does the problem lie?

Yes: I've provided numerous examples in the book of the ways we plant and feed conflict that would otherwise never germinate. Hooks are powerful. They get us into trouble sometimes. They sure get me into trouble sometimes, and I desperately hope I'm not alone.

4
What if someone is trying to press my buttons?

We use the phrase "he knows just how to press my buttons" to mean that someone knows how to aggravate or provoke a reaction from us. The feeling of getting our buttons pushed can range from mild irritation to strong anger, from Bad Tammy opening one eye in faint interest to sirens shrieking a threat level of DEFCON 1.

While we say, "She's pressing my buttons," it would be more accurate to say, "I've managed to get hooked by something she said." While the first places responsibility on the act of someone else, the second rightfully acknowledges that you are at least an equal partner in your own button pressing—and perhaps the only one responsible.

Hooks and buttons are essentially the same. I prefer the term *hooks* because it conveys something inside us that gets snagged, instead of *buttons*, which conveys that someone outside us must press them.

Someone cannot press your buttons without your consent. Remember the old master in chapter 4: "If someone comes to give you a gift and you do not receive it," the master replied, "to whom does the gift belong?" Knowledge of your conflict hooks and how to manage them gives you the ability to keep your calm when someone bears the gift of insults (or presses your buttons).

I don't believe someone gets out of bed in the morning planning how to press your buttons. It's more likely that people are going about their business and inadvertently stumble into your conflict hooks. Or that they felt provoked by you after you stumbled into their conflict hooks and now they're reciprocating the "favor." Either way, you are now or have been in the past a partner in this.

5

Are you saying that inner work is the answer to all my conflict problems?

No. There is no single answer to all conflict problems. There are certainly interpersonal conflict situations in which even the most self-responsible, self-aware, and self-actualized among us would still come up short by relying solely on inner work. To paraphrase architect Christopher Alexander,[1] your state of harmony does sometimes rely on harmony not just from within, but also on harmony with what's around you.

You knew there was a "but" coming, didn't you? Here you go, then: but in nearly twenty years of conflict resolution work, I've seen too many people significantly over-rely on what the other person will or won't do and under-rely on inner work as a way to change their relationship with conflict that is plaguing them.

There is terrific power in the right inner work done well. The pivots are all thought processes, all inner work. Sometimes, maybe most times, that will be all you need. Sometimes, they will prepare you for the "outer work" that must come. That is, sometimes the pivots' best outcome is to make sure you're having a conversation with the other person about the right things, the things that will truly make a difference in helping you move forward.

6

But I know my stuck story is right.

In the late 1990s I was one of a handful of mediators chosen to test a new online mediation platform for eBay. Online dispute resolution, or ODR, was in its infancy and we were learning and providing feedback on the software and experience as we went. The disputants were located all over the world—wherever eBay purchases and sales could be made—and I mediated the disputes from my New Hampshire office.

One case involved some apparently missing charms. I'd replied to the young woman who filed the case, asking for more information about what had happened with her eBay purchase. I had written, "What do you mean when you say you don't have the charms you paid for? Did they just fall off or something?"

She wrote back, "LOOK, THE CHARMS JUST DISAPPEARED? OK? THAT'S ALL THERE IS TO SAY!"

I stared at the capital letters, wondering if she normally typed with caps lock on or if she was yelling toward me in frustration. Pondering the all-caps response, I typed, "I'm clearly missing something here. They just disappeared? I don't get it yet, please tell me more."

Several hours later came her next reply: "ARE YOU AN IDIOT? LOOK, I WENT TO THE CAVES, I FOUGHT THE DEMONS, I LOST POWER, SO I BOUGHT THE CHARMS SO I'D HAVE POWER AGAIN AND THEN THEY JUST DISAPPEARED. SHE SCAMMED ME AND I WANT MY MONEY BACK. COMPRENDE?"

And you are still fighting the demons, I thought to myself, throwing my hands into the air, simultaneously acting out my despair and supplicating the heavens for aid.

Then it hit me. "We're not talking about charms for a charm bracelet," I typed, dating myself. "We're talking charms for an online fantasy game? Not physical charms but digital ones?"

"DUH!" she wrote back almost instantly.

So easy to judge, so seductive to diagnose, so tantalizing to think we're the ones with the right understanding of the story. And, as a result, so easy to miss the real story unless we give ourselves permission not to know and be open to what we're missing.

So, it is important to distinguish having a thought from believing it. It is important to be aware of all the ways you nurture your stuck story and cause it to feel like the "real" one, as I discussed in chapter 3. Interfaith minister and meditation teacher Allan Lokos encourages us not to confuse thoughts, feelings, and perceptions with reality. He says, "Practice seeing things as they really are. Don't believe everything you think. Thoughts are just that—thoughts. They are not reality."[2]

One of my graduate students, Jaclyn, said it this way: "[Now] I'm able to be witness to my thought, which keeps the trickery of my mind in check and in place."

7

But everyone agrees with me about the other person.

Sometimes, we're so hooked by our identity fears that we find it soothing to feel part of a crowd. I had this experience as I worked on pivoting during the website copying incident. As I was starting the third pivot, my inner narrator kept saying, "Expecting him to undo what he did is not unreasonable. If you walked down the street and told ten people your story, nine of them would say that you are right to confront him and make him see the error of his ways." My conflict hooks were building their defense force by showing me that "everyone" would see it my way. My hooks were telling me I wasn't alone, that "everyone" would think similarly. My hooks were keeping me snagged by making me feel justified.

We do this in conflict. We say, "Well, everyone in the office thinks he's a jerk." We say, "The children all see her bad temper and want to live with me." We say, "Everyone on the committee agrees that he's very passive-aggressive." Allies make us feel stronger, more right, and more righteous.

They can also keep us quite stuck. They cause us to conflate supporting with endorsing. Your allies may be trying to support you, as I was supporting my friend who felt righteous anger about bad treatment from a court employee (see chapter 3). Sometimes people trying to be supportive sound like they agree with you because they have only your version of what happened to inform them.

When I was in graduate school, the curriculum required a course in ethics. I kept putting off registering for the course because of the horror stories fellow students told about the professor. They told war stories about Dr. Nash's ability to make them feel stupid with his difficult questions, about how impossible it was to succeed in the course, and about how much pleasure he seemed to take in his students' misery. Eventually I could put off taking the course no longer. On the first day of class, Dr. Nash's reputation did seem to be no exaggeration. I went home quaking in my boots, which I suspected he wanted us all to be doing.

On the way to the second class, it occurred to me that Dr. Nash might not be relishing his students' fear at all. It occurred to me that Dr. Nash might believe that by pushing us, he was helping us rise to a new level. I decided to sit in class with that frame of mind, if only so I didn't feel anxious all through class. It paid off. The course was difficult, yes, but I found I relished it. To this day, I remember my ethics course as one of the best courses I ever took, and Dr. Nash as one of the best teachers I've ever known. Dr. Nash had been no different than he'd ever been. The only thing that changed was the way I chose to think about the professor.

Regardless of what others around you think, you still have to interact with your colleague, report to your supervisor, make decisions with your fellow committee chair. What "everyone" else thinks doesn't, if you'll pardon the pun, let you off the hook at all. If you wait for "everyone" to fix this for you, you may well have a long wait, during which your own performance is also being observed and evaluated.

I recommend you stop using the figurative masses to help you avoid your own discomfort, make discomfort your ally instead, and spend your energy sorting out how you will address the state of tension between you and the other person.

8
How can I unhook myself when the identity insult really is intended?

Here are my favorite ways:

Beware of totalizing. Check in with yourself and make sure you are not totalizing the remark (see chapter 5 for a refresher on totalizing, the experience of viewing something through an all-or-nothing lens).

Play it through to its logical conclusion. One way you can unhook yourself from the time- and energy-sucking practice of defending your identity against even the smallest insults is to follow the perceived insult to its logical conclusion. For instance, if you perceive that the Mobil station attendant thinks you're an incompetent gas pumper, follow that to its logical conclusion: What if it's true that he does think that? What if he is right? How much does that matter in my life/for my job/in this relationship? Some perceived identity insults become positively humorous when you follow them to their logical conclusion, and then it is easier to let them go.

Consider the source. My husband is very good at shrugging off identity insults from people he'll never see again or whose opinion he doesn't value much. I have to work a bit harder to do that, but I do try because it's a very good practice. If the source of the true identity insult is one that doesn't matter to you or is one that perhaps enjoys your discomfort (the latter is rarer than you are tempted to conclude), then it's very freeing to be able to shrug it off. If you have to say something in response, you can say simply, "Thanks for the feedback. I'll consider it." You see, considering feedback and agreeing with it are different things, and you need not tangle with them about it.

Trade defensiveness for transparency. Sometimes the identity insult contains enough truth that it warrants you bringing it up for discussion. Imagine, for instance, that you have a strong fellowship hook. Your supervisor shares her written feedback for your annual performance review, and in it she states that you need to be more of a team player on a key project. It's likely you'd have a strong reaction to this, perhaps even fail to notice all the other positive comments in the performance appraisal (which would be a very totalizing thing to do). You may defend yourself heartily and lay out all the reasons that you've been thwarted from being the kind of team player you know yourself to be.

Try being transparent instead of defensive. Say to your supervisor, "I like to think of myself as a strong team player and it really jolts me that you don't see me that way. It would help me to understand what you're seeing that leads you to conclude that about me." Then be quiet. Wait for her to reply fully. Don't defend. Don't interrupt. Just listen. See what you find out. You may discover that your supervisor is missing key information, which you will now have the opportunity to provide. You may discover your supervisor has some valid points, and you haven't been as strong a team player as you thought. If the latter, you'll emerge from the conversation knowing what you need to do. The world will not stop rotating.

In many instances it is useful to check out the perceived threat instead of dismissing it out of hand or acting on it as though it is genuine. You may recall the way I checked out the perceived identity insult at the Mobil station. After he muttered something about the pump working just a few minutes before, I asked him, "What do you mean?"

I've found that the question "What do you mean?" is excellent for checking out perceived identity threats and insults. It invites additional information without leading the other person to a specific answer. Of course, the intention with which you ask this question will have an impact on its success. If you mean to communicate your dislike of their comments, your simple question will come out as though you have one hand on your hip and are copping an attitude. If you mean to communicate defiance, your question will come out as though you've got both hands on your hips like an angry parent. "What do you mean?" is a powerful question for checking out perceived identity insults when asked with an attitude of true curiosity.

Another way to check out the perceived threat is to name the threat you picked up on and confirm their intention. For instance, I could have said to the Mobil station attendant, perhaps with a smile that reflected the half-joking question, "Are you saying that I'm an inept Speedpass user?"

9

What if the other person really doesn't see me the way I see myself?

These are some of the most emotionally difficult situations. When they happen with people we care about or need to work with, they rock our world. Yet, there is something to latch onto, something you didn't have before: clarity.

Imagine that Eva, the woman who ran a farm with her husband, approached her husband as I suggested in chapter 5. With an approach like this, Eva is taking a courageous step by asking about the thing she fears most. Instead of continuing the back and forth of differing opinions about the farm's future, she is acknowledging how the conflict has hooked her and is asking for clarity from her husband. Did he really mean her opinion didn't matter to him, or had the comment come out of the heat of his anger? To what degree did he believe she should have a role in the decision making? To what degree did he value what she valued in herself, her helpfulness and cooperation over thirty-five years of farm work?

Identity conversations like these can feel frightening to broach. They feel frightening because we lay ourselves bare with loved ones or with colleagues. They feel frightening because we risk their taking advantage of us after we've shown our cards. They feel frightening because they may tell us they don't value in us what we value in ourselves, and then the very foundations of a relationship may be shaken. It is possible, after all, that Eva's husband, even when calm and fully in charge of himself, may tell her that his family's long history on the farm matters more to him than her thirty-five years of contribution. It would surely rock Eva's world to hear this.

I view difficult news like this as better than pretending, better than arguing over the presenting problem instead of the real and true problem. Because if Eva and her husband have spent thirty-five years with very different feelings about their respective roles on, ownership of, and dedication to their farm, they most certainly have a problem that is overdue for attention.

There is also this: if Eva's husband were to confirm her greatest identity fear—that her fellowship doesn't matter as much to him as she wants it to—then Eva will know what she is working with. She will know that the decision about the farm may not reflect her wishes fully. She will know that her view of the farm partnership with her husband is quite different from her husband's. She will have to figure out what that means for their remaining years together.

This is the stuff of sleepless nights, yes. It is also the stuff of clarity and, much later, freedom. If Eva and her husband do not deal with the real and true problem between them, that problem does not go away. Like a pebble thrown into a still pond, it will send ripples throughout the marriage and into every challenging decision they have to make.

10
Do the pivots allow us to let ourselves off the hook too easily?

A colleague challenged me with this question,

suggesting that it's possible for people to act badly, perhaps very badly, and then use the pivots to find their own peace of mind and move on. In that scenario they would be letting themselves off the hook while still leaving "relational debris" in their wake.

It seems to me that someone who cares so little for how others are feeling can find a way to use almost any conflict resolution approach superficially to serve his or her own desires. There is no foolproof approach for beings as complicated as we are.

That said, the pivots are intended to achieve exactly the opposite outcome. I created them to help you take a careful look inside and to stop blaming the other person for the ways the conflict has hooked and weighed on you. The pivots ask you to *stop* letting yourself off the hook by externalizing the conflict and instead to start recognizing the conflict experience as something living in your core.

11

Aren't the conflict pivots just a fancy form of avoidance?

If you pivot well, it's the opposite of avoidance: you are addressing the conflict by figuring out what's hooked you, why, and which options are best for dealing with it. You may choose to let it go or you may choose to talk it out.

Avoidance is the choice not to address a conflict. Avoidance can be a problem, though it is not always so. For instance, if it is your default habit in conflict, avoidance can drain you of power and influence because your voice is not part of the solution. If a conflict is truly important and you avoid it, it probably does not go away. A simmering, unresolved conflict can create bigger problems for you later or alienate you from someone important in your life.

Some conflicts warrant avoidance. Conflicts that are minor skirmishes with people you won't see again or who don't have much role in your life may be better served with avoidance because it's not worth your energy, and you can learn to let these go.

Your oversensitive conflict hooks cause some conflicts. In these instances, you don't want to avoid the self-work of dealing with these conflicts but can rightfully avoid confrontation or discussion.

12

Isn't this just about putting spit and polish on a bad situation?

Conflict pivots are not about trying to view a stressful situation in a more positive light, an approach called cognitive reappraisal.

Cognitive reappraisal is a strategy that involves reframing your negative thoughts about a given situation in order to change its emotional impact on you.[3] While the conflict pivots do invite you to reframe your thoughts about the situation or the other person, the goal isn't to see the situation in a more positive light. The goal of the pivots is to help you uncover what the conflict is really about for you and to help you identify fruitful options for dealing with it and other conflicts like it in the future.

13
Why didn't my pivots "stick"?

Recently a woman said to me, "When I work through the pivots, I feel good about the result to let it go and move on. But when I see the other person again, I revert back to my old way of thinking. Why don't my pivots last?"

Imagine that you have a friend named Martin. If you've concluded Martin is passive-aggressive, you will have a tendency to notice the things he does that fit your diagnosis of his flaws. This is called a reflexive loop. Reflexive loops are caused when you select partial data from your observations, draw conclusions as a result of the selected data, and use those conclusions to generate a belief about the person or situation. Your belief then affects what data you notice next time, creating a loop in your thinking and further feeding your belief.[4] It's a tandem idea to a self-fulfilling prophecy.

Things are further complicated by the ways your perception is influenced by your imagination. While you may believe that you can differentiate between what you imagine and what you actually see and hear, reality is not so clear cut. What you imagine hearing can change what you actually see, and what you imagine seeing can change what you actually hear. Let me repeat that. What you actually see can be changed by what you imagine hearing, and what you actually hear can be changed by what you imagine seeing. Sensory signals generated by your imagination are strong enough to change your real-world perceptions.[5]

If you practice your narrow conclusions and misbegotten beliefs simply by allowing them to continue, they start to feel like The Truth about Martin. Your diagnosis of his flaw continues, unchallenged, because you are inadvertently filtering out data that doesn't support your conclusion about him and noticing the data that does.

Then you pivot and you now have a new understanding of the dynamic between you and Martin. It's a helpful new view but not yet so well rehearsed as your old stuck story. So it will be easy for you to revert to your familiar stuck story when you see Martin next. He'll do something, and your inner narrator will shout gleefully, "See! I knew it! Classic passive-aggressive, if ever there was one."

If you care more about your freedom from the conflict than you do about the ego-soothing voice in your head, then you have to negotiate with yourself. You must give your new awareness time to prove itself, and, during that period, you must prevent it from being nudged aside by your old stuck story.

14
What about dealing with difficult people?

There are no difficult people. There are people who seem difficult to *you*. Remember this very wise Kottler quote I shared earlier in the book: "Every person you fight with has many other people in his life with whom he gets along quite well. You cannot look at a person who seems difficult to you without also looking at yourself."

When you say, "He is a difficult person," you have made "being difficult" part of the fabric of his being, part of who he is as a human. You've also put him in a box, and people don't usually take very well to being put in boxes. It makes them, well, difficult.

Try these on your tongue instead: "I find him difficult." "He is acting very difficult right now." "He has some difficult behaviors." "Our team finds her behavior a challenge for us."

When you frame the difficulty you're experiencing in these ways, you set yourself up for the kind of inquiry a masterful mediator knows to ask next: "What is it in the environment (or in my supervision, or my interactions with, or the organizational change, or about his job duties) that's contributing to the difficult behaviors?" Or, "How is our dynamic together making this more difficult?"

You're not done yet, though. If there's a "difficult person" in your life, you must next ask yourself, "What is hooking me?"

15
Is this like cognitive behavior therapy?

Since I am not a therapist, I cannot tell you from experience how similar or dissimilar the conflict pivots are to cognitive behavior therapy, or CBT. From reading about CBT, I can see that there are a few philosophical underpinnings that both approaches have in common:

- They place less emphasis on the past and more on changing the now.
- They help you reconsider how you're thinking about a problem (cognition) so that you can respond differently (behavior).
- They teach how to be more consciously aware of

your thinking so that you're in a better position to choose your response.

- They favor introspective individuals who are willing to be flexible in their thinking about a problem.

Beyond those philosophical similarities, CBT and conflict pivots diverge. While CBT is a therapeutic approach administered by a psychotherapist with her patient, conflict pivots are not psychotherapy; they are self-guided questions to help you think about a specific conflict in new ways. Cognitive behavior therapy, of which there are several types, typically has a specific sequence of steps that are quite different from the pivots and is typically a process that takes place over many hours.

16

Can I use the pivots in conflicts that involve more than one other person?

Yes. To make this book's examples easier to digest and learn, I often described conflict involving only two people. But there is nothing about the pivots that makes them useful only in situations where you are in conflict with a single individual. Since the conflict pivots are a way for you to better grasp the reasons a conflict is eating at you and to discover better paths out of conflict, you can readily use the practices in conflicts within families, workplace teams, boards of directors, committees, and the like.

17

How big a conflict can make use of the pivots?

Large-scale conflict scholar Jay Rothman focuses his work on identity-based conflict, most notably conflict resolution between Jews and Arabs in Israel. Rothman describes identity-based conflict as rooted in our psychology, culture, beliefs, basic values, and shared history. He points out that identity-based conflicts are often mistaken for disputes over material resources because resource issues are concrete and can be clearly defined, while identity-based conflicts tend to be abstract and ambiguous. Identity conflicts, says Rothman, engage strong passions and can lead to great destruction.[6]

Our identities are powerful and deep, the glue that binds us and a source of some of our most painful divides. Identity powers international conflict, community conflict, organizational conflict, and family conflict. It powers conflicts between two countries and conflicts between two people.

I created the pivots for individuals to address important conflict that has them stuck and to move past unimportant conflict that would otherwise weigh them down. You can use the pivots to change the form of a conflict in your family, in your organization, or among your friends or your neighbors. Pivot well and you may never know what destruction you avoided by choosing to change the way you responded to a conflict.

Historian and social activist Howard Zinn said, "Every word you utter to another human being has an effect. But you don't know it. If people began to understand that change comes about as a result of millions of tiny acts that seem totally insignificant, well, then, they wouldn't hesitate to take those tiny acts."[7]

Conflict pivots are some of those tiny acts.

7

THE PIVOTING HABIT

When you began the conflict pivots journey, your stuck
story shaped your view of the conflict and what was
needed to resolve it. Like a movie trailer, your stuck story
was a montage of moments that most held your attention;
you ignored or omitted other scenes entirely. Now you
know why those moments held your attention.

Now you have turned away from your stuck story and
toward the message it has held for you. You have learned
to listen for the message and you have uncovered your
conflict hooks. You have pivoted away from dwelling on
the past and toward a future in which you have the power
to transform the conflict into peace of mind.

You are rewriting the story of your conflict.

But knowledge alone may well fail you. You may
know your stuck story is an incomplete and biased story
of your conflict, but that awareness doesn't get you very
far if you don't do anything with it. You may see that an
important part of what hooks you in conflict is your own
fragile identity, which your unconscious self may go
overboard to protect. But that knowledge won't get you

very far if you let your old habits drive your responses during conflict.

Earlier in the book I shared Jeffrey Kottler's observation that people who have been in therapy for years can still find themselves "enlightened wrecks" because understanding past mistakes doesn't automatically lead to avoiding them. Over many years of teaching conflict resolution and negotiation to graduate students, I've seen a similar phenomenon. I've had the good fortune to work with countless students who reveled in gaining new knowledge and new self-knowledge; this is in many ways a professor's dream. At the same time, I've observed how difficult some of those same students found it to bridge the gap between insight and application, between knowing and doing.

While teaching a negotiation course for a master's program in healthcare administration, I required students to negotiate something monetary and something relational every single week of the seven-week course. Initially, most students found this a daunting assignment, even though they were all middle- and upper-level managers who were already negotiating informally throughout their workdays. At first, I couldn't understand why my assignment seemed like such a challenge to them, given their daily work responsibilities. Then I understood: I wasn't asking them to do what they always did; I was asking them to take their new negotiation knowledge from class and apply it. Old habits were easy for them; trying to create new ones felt riskier.

Of course, since this was a class assignment, it turned out to be a very good mechanism to entice follow-through from these students. They had to have their small negotiations, then report on them and discuss them in class. They couldn't really get out of the discomfort of this assignment without also choosing to fail the course.

Here is what happened: There were a couple of students who kept claiming to be turning classroom knowledge into practical application at home or work, but who could not demonstrate that their negotiations reflected this claim. I only saw them falling back on old habits when negotiating, and these students emerged from the course with little real learning. Perhaps it goes without saying that they also emerged from the course with lower grades, because they also couldn't demonstrate facility with key course ideas.

The vast majority of the students, though, did take the new information and tried to apply it in small weekly negotiations. They floundered a bit at first, but in a short time they found that not only did they successfully negotiate things they didn't think they could, but these negotiations were growing easier to undertake. They put their knowledge to practice haltingly at first, but over time their fluency with the ideas began to increase.

So it will be with the conflict pivots if you expect something about your conflicts to change. Ben Franklin, well known for his commitment to self-improvement, wrote that he asked himself a question each morning: "What good shall I do this day?" and its bookend question each evening: "What good have I done today?"[1] I see these questions as his very fine mechanism for translating his self-improvement ideas into action.

Linda, whom we've followed throughout the book, put her insights to work, too. Once she realized how many of her real goals she could achieve on her own, she decided that the conversation she most wanted to have with her brother was one in which they could explore the tension between them, with as little defensiveness as possible, and figure out how to begin rebuilding the relationships she had once so treasured.

Linda told her brother that she was aware of the widening gap between them and had been pondering some of the reasons. She told him about her conflict hooks and the ways she experienced his decisions as ways to exploit her reliability. She explained the work she had undertaken to unhook herself. She told him that she wanted to share with him the things she most wanted for herself from here forward and talk about what he most wanted for himself. They had the kind of heart-to-heart she'd been yearning for as long as she could remember.

Issues related to her father's care did not get resolved in this conversation; Linda, in fact, steered the conversation away from those issues for now. She knew that if she and her brother could reduce the tension between them, they could deal with those issues more successfully later. And she knew, of course, that she already had a viable path to achieve her own peace of mind, independent of her brother's decisions.

In our last conversation, Linda said to me, "Early in our time together you told me it only takes one to change the dance. I didn't believe you. But this weekend, I changed my dance steps, and I think I changed my life."

Make These Practices Your Own

The conflict pivot practices are a type of scaffolding, not unlike the staging used by housepainters to reach heights their brushes could not otherwise touch. The conflict pivot scaffolding is a temporary framework put up for support and for access to places you might not reach without it. You will not need each question of each pivot forever, though you may well occasionally wish to pull all the scaffolding back out and use it to touch up your thinking about a certain conflict.

You don't need each piece of the scaffolding forever because with a little bit of practice, the pivots can become habit, a way to gain access to your best self when you need him or her most. You don't need all the scaffolding forever because once you have a grasp of the basics, you will not need every single plank to keep you safe and steady. You don't need all the scaffolding forever because as you practice the pivots, you will probably modify the scaffolding, changing its setup and design to make it work best for your needs and to reach new heights.

Make these practices your own.

Practice in Low-Stakes Situations

I began to cross-country ski while in college, but I didn't bother to take any lessons until I was in my late twenties. In the years between I kept to low-elevation, green diamond trails, and when I needed to stop, my pace was usually slow enough that I could just lean over into a snow bank without hurting myself. I was just puttering around.

When I met my husband, also a tenderfoot cross-country skier, we decided we wanted to be able to ski down some of Stowe, Vermont's, best Nordic trails. We wanted to climb up Trapp Family Lodge's Cabin Trail and then fly down the Old Haul Road. We wanted to climb to the very top of Edson Hill's trail network and then shush down through the acres of sunny meadows that were there at the time. We knew we needed some lessons.

Our instructor did not, mercifully, take us to the top

of the mountain and say, "This is how you stop. Got it? Ok, go on, have fun, see you at the bottom. Try not to hit any trees on your way down." Instead, she took us to a gradual slope at the Sherman Hollow ski touring center near where we lived and taught us a variety of ways to control our speed, change direction, stop, and the like. My husband and I practiced many green and blue diamond trails before we eventually made our first foray up to the Old Haul Road at Trapp's. It was only much later that we'd race to the bottom of the Old Haul Road on our cross-country skis, whooping with joy and trying to get up as much speed as possible. We knew by then that we could control our direction and stop without colliding with the lodge at the bottom.

So it is with conflict pivots. Practice pivoting in low-stakes situations, those Mobil station moments that cause minor identity quakes. Practice like this helps you become more familiar with your hooks and the subtle ways they snag you. I call the conflict pivots "practices" for a reason, you know. You'll build your muscle memory for the high-stakes situations. You might even whoop for joy.

Don't Fear the Groan Zone

Even when you've done your best pivoting, a conflict can still feel messy or daunting to sort out. Your task in those moments is not to let your fear of the groan zone deter you.

Fibber McGee and Molly was a popular radio show in the United States from the 1930s to the 1950s and featured real-life husband and wife Jim Jordan and Marian Driscoll as the main characters. Fibber McGee had an overstuffed, junk-filled closet that was "just the way" he liked it. His wife, Molly, tried in vain to get Fibber to clean out the closet. Whichever unfortunate soul—it might be Molly, Fibber, or a visitor—opened the closet door would find items raining down on their heads and spilling out onto the floor around them. The "Fibber McGee's closet" gag was so popular that the phrase "like opening Fibber McGee's closet" became synonymous with bringing up messy matters.

The groan zone in a conflict is a little like having opened Fibber McGee's closet. You've courageously opened the door of the conflict. Things begin to tumble out at you, perhaps faster than you can absorb. Some of the things that tumble out may not have seen the light of day for quite a while; others figuratively hit you in the head with such great force you see stars for a moment. It's easy to stare at the mess in front of you and find even your best hopes quaking in their shoes.

Consensus decision-making expert Sam Kaner coined the term *groan zone*,[2] and it's an apt phrase for the messy stage. Too often, fear of the groan zone causes teams, groups, families, and couples to hurry past it. Most head straight into problem solving in an attempt to get away from discomfort and feeling overwhelmed by retreating to the apparent safety of solution generating. I see this tendency particularly prevalent in workplace teams, perhaps hurrying past their discomfort in a misguided bid to prevent interpersonal tension.

The real misfortune of this approach is that, without the kind of understanding that comes from slowing down and taking a real look at each of the items that came spilling out, the solutions generated aren't as strong and useful as they otherwise would be. Hurrying through the groan zone is a mistake because that's where the real heart of the difficult conversation lies. It's where some of the best learning, thinking, understanding, and creativity have their genesis.

When you find yourself in the groan zone, don't hurry past. Don't try to cram all the items back in the closet and slam the door closed again. Look at what's in front of you. Pick one up and examine it closely. Talk about it. Make sure you understand it. Only then move on to the next item.

The best way to navigate the groan zone is the best way, as they say, to eat an elephant: one bite at a time.

Pivot Early; Pivot Often

Pivot early; pivot often.

Don't wait until the conflict is onerous to pivot. One benefit of pivoting early in a real and true conflict is that your stuck story is not well rehearsed and you're not deeply committed to it yet.

As I was writing this book, I experienced tension with a woman who served on a volunteer committee with me. Early in the committee work, I noted that Anne seemed to drop the ball a lot. She missed agreed-upon deadlines set by the committee chair, and she didn't have much to offer during progress reports. I'd already begun forming an opinion about her even though her problems didn't have any impact on my work. My story about her was becoming stuck even when it didn't matter to me.

But one day, it did matter to me. Anne did something I experienced as very underhanded. It ticked me off. In fact, it ticked me off enough that I sat right down with a piece of paper and worked out the three pivots. This was a woman I would continue to run into, and I didn't want tension to rule those moments. I also didn't want my energy sapped during a very busy period at work. I wanted to be free of the tension right away, before it became chronic. Here's what I wrote, hammered out in about five minutes in short-form pivots:

What is my stuck story about Anne?

- She's a slacker.
- She's passive-aggressive, getting her way by doing what she wants instead of collaborating.
- She's secretive and manipulative, so I can't trust her.

Why do I care? What does my stuck story tell me about why this is bothering me?

- Autonomy hook: I don't like feeling manipulated.
- Status hook: I don't like that she could do a poor job on a project that could ultimately reflect on me.
- Competence hook, tinged with a bit of inclusion hook: I don't like my intelligence being insulted by her. Did she think I'm too dumb or too oblivious to find out what she did?

What do I want for myself in this situation from here forward and what will I do about it?

- I'm realizing I don't really care if Anne is trying to manipulate me. In five years I'll barely register her presence in my life this year. Let me put my energy where it matters.
- It's ridiculous for me to think that her poor work

will reflect poorly on me. People will know my work for what it is and hers for what it is. I can let this one go; it's a red herring.

- I'm realizing what's most eating at me is her dismissal of my contribution. Do I care enough about this that it's worth continuing to address this with her? No, I don't. If she wants to believe that, I'm ok with it. It does not damage my life in any way. The only thing that damages my life is letting my hooks lead my thoughts and cause me to dwell on her behavior.

At the bottom of the paper, I wrote: "I'm done with this. I'm letting it go. It doesn't warrant any more of my energy." I continued to see Anne now and then. At first, when she said or did something that my hooked self would have basked in, my unhooked self had to remind me to shrug and let others who cared deal with it. We exchanged pleasantries, even joked a few times. She was not my best friend, but neither did she feel like the enemy or like someone whose presence irked me.

By pivoting early, before my irritation with Anne became cemented, I was able to free myself from the irritation and move on. Extricating yourself from an unimportant trouble spot is well within your means now, too.

Pivot early; pivot often.

From Here Forward

After losing someone she loved and going through a long period of grief, experimental artist Candy Chang painted the side of an abandoned house in New Orleans with chalkboard paint and stenciled the chalkboard repeatedly with the words, "Before I die I want to ____." She left chalk in many colors. By the next day, the wall was completely filled with a rainbow of hopes and dreams, contemplations of death that reminded people what they cared most about in life.

What began as an experiment has lead to something akin to an art movement: over 450 walls have been created in thirty languages in over sixty-five countries, including Halifax, Nova Scotia, where my husband and I happened upon one of the walls. Chang's exploration of death, grief, life, and hope has touched thousands.

People's comments on the Before I Die walls reflect the diverse tapestry of humanity, from insightful to playful, joyous to sad, mundane to outrageous. Some comments convey a longing for connection and reconnection and for peace of mind. Chang has recorded responses like these:[3]

"Before I die I want to forgive and be forgiven"— Chicago, Illinois, United States

"Antes de morir yo quiero tener la armonía y la salud (Before I die I want to have harmony and health)"— Bogotá, Colombia

"Before I die I want to forgive my father"—Be'er Sheva, Israel

"Before I die I want to have more presence, less panic"—Rutland, Vermont, United States

"Before I die I want to ask for forgiveness"—Nilai, Malaysia

"Before I die I want to heal"—Montréal, Quebec, Canada

"Before I die I want to find closure"—Erfurt, Germany

"Before I die I want to sort out my life"—Kladno, Czech Republic

"Before I die I want to live with more joy"—Nelson, New Zealand

These are moving reminders that our relationships are among the most important things in our lives. They are reminders that healing, peace of mind, and joy are deeply important, even if we occasionally lose sight of them in the daily hubbub. They are reminders that the only time over which we have true dominion is right now, for who knows how many hours or days or years are left for each of us?

Take the time now to pivot. Take the time now to discover what your conflicts are trying to tell you. Take the time now to learn how to ignore the false alarms in your everyday life, creating space for more joy to take root. Take the time now to strengthen your professional and business relationships and to deepen and enrich your connection with loved ones. These are your most important pursuits, the ones that matter, the ones in which hope and joy live.

ACKNOWLEDGEMENTS

This book stands on the shoulders of giants. Rosamund and Benjamin Zander, along with the father of Appreciative Inquiry, David Cooperrider, caused me to fall in love with the art of possibility. Susan Terry, Alice Estey, and David Specht taught me the power of good questions, and Byron Katie's work showed me the power of a few well-chosen ones. Thomas Moore's books taught me to write deeply from the heart. Jason Fried's books reminded me to write courageously and straightforwardly whenever self-doubt began to fray me at the edges. The people behind the Public Conversations Project taught me that the power of insight may well be more important than the power of resolution. Jeffrey Kottler's and Jay Rothman's work introduced me to the ways that identity shapes conflict, and Stella Ting-Toomey's domains gave me the gift of clear, straightforward language to talk about identity and conflict. Isaac Asimov taught me to see beyond what I expect to see. Without these giants, the conflict pivots would not exist.

My deep gratitude also goes to the many dozens of graduate students and unnamed clients (you know who you are) in whose service the conflict pivots saw the first seeds sowed. Thank you to Jen Otis for an elegantly frank appraisal of my textbook choices in class, Kregg Nance for asking a simple question that sent me on a long quest, and Jaclyn Mothupi, Taryn Hill, and Adele Simons for exquisite quotes. Those of you who have learned from me should know that I have learned equally much—perhaps more—from you. And that is as it should be, the right and proper dance of teaching and learning.

Nan Starr, Jeanne Cleary, and my sister Pepi Noble gave much of themselves and their smarts as generous readers of early drafts. It is a far better book for their unflinching and loving feedback. Readers of my conflict resolution blog also read many parts of this book in short form, as I tested out ideas over the past decade. Their comments helped me see what resonated and what didn't and had an indelible impact on the book.

I am most fortunate to be related to the director Matt Lenski and that he was willing to give of himself and his talent to bring this book's trailer to life. I'm lucky, too, that Brian Caiazza and Jen Watts of Goodlookin' were willing to partner with Matt and do such damn smart work with the animation and production. So much talent and such good people all.

In the movie *Shall We Dance?* Susan Sarandon's character said, "We need a witness to our lives. There's [*sic*] a billion people on the planet, what does any one life really mean? But in a marriage, you're promising to care about everything. The good things, the bad things, the terrible things, the mundane things, all of it, all of the time, every day. You're saying, 'Your life will not go unnoticed because I will notice it. Your life will not go unwitnessed because I will be your witness."' I met my husband, Rod, in 1989, and he is both my life's witness and this book's witness. His support, his willingness to be a guinea pig, his feedback, and his loving kindness helped me make a better book and cherish him all the more. Rod, as Yoda would say: Good man, you are.

ABOUT THE AUTHOR

Dr. Tammy Lenski, EdD, helps individuals, teams, and couples develop everyday conflict resolution practices that lead to sound business and personal relationships. She has consulted, mediated, coached, and trained for more than twenty years. Tammy was one of the founding faculty of Champlain College's graduate program in mediation and applied conflict studies. A member of the Association for Conflict Resolution's Academy of Advanced Practitioners, she received the association's prestigious 2012 Mary Parker Follett award for innovative and pioneering work in the conflict resolution field. Tammy's home on the web is lenski.com, where she's blogged about conflict and resolution since 2002. She lives in New Hampshire with her husband, two rescue dogs, and an inscrutable cat.

APPENDIX
CONFLICT PIVOT ESSENTIALS

The following is a quick reference guide to *The Conflict Pivot*. It's useful for giving you a view of the forest after your walk through the trees, so to speak. It's also useful for reminding you later of essential conflict pivot ideas and practices.

The Definition and Purpose of a Conflict Pivot

A conflict pivot is a purposeful change in the direction you're focusing during conflict in order to achieve better results.

Pivoting is a thought process. Many conflict resolution approaches are interactional, meaning they focus on the way people in conflict interact, or interpersonal, meaning that they focus on the way people relate and communicate in conflict. Pivoting is intrapersonal, meaning that it takes place inside your own mind.

The Power of Pivoting

The conflict pivots help you dissolve conflict in ongoing personal and professional relationships by giving you effective alternatives to what you're doing now.

They help you achieve results like the following:

- Discern why a conflict snagged your attention, why you remain snagged, and how to unhook yourself from the conflict.
- Identify the most common reasons you get snagged by conflict and replace habits doomed to get you stuck with habits that help set you free.
- Simplify what you need to remember in order to navigate a conflict effectively.
- Prevent some conflict from occurring at all.
- Truly let go and move on from some conflicts.
- Discern precisely what you should discuss with the other person so that real resolution is within your grasp.
- Break cycles of blame and resentment.
- Take back the power you have to resolve a conflict without relying on what the other person will or won't do.

The Guiding Principles in Brief

The conflict pivots have their foundation in the following guiding principles. It is important to be aware of these guiding principles because if they don't resonate with you, the practice of pivoting may feel hollow to you.

- **Your story of the conflict is not *the* story of the conflict**, any more than the other person's story is. Your story of the conflict is a partial story of what happened, a montage of the moments that most snagged your attention. When you "rehearse" your story by telling it to others or yourself, it becomes "stuck" as you replay it; these are called Stuck Stories. To resolve the conflict effectively, you must stop rehearsing your stuck story and instead understand what that story is trying to tell you.

- **The source of your discomfort is inside you.** When you are in conflict with someone and you experience pain or frustration, you may look to that person as the cause of your discomfort. You would do better to look within. You are feeling discomfort for a reason, and when you discern the reason, you have an important key for unlocking the conflict.

- **Relief comes from here forward, not from the past.** Rehashing what happened, who did what to whom, who was wrong, and the like, can trap you in conflict because you cannot change what happened. You can only change how you view it and what you're going to do from here forward to free yourself.

- **Complicated stuff doesn't need more complication.** Human nature is complex. Conflict is complex. Conflict resolution shouldn't have to be.

- **Release from conflict can be a solo act.** "Conflict resolution" is generally understood as a collaborative activity involving discussion and negotiation with the other person. Yet it is possible, sometimes even preferable, to resolve a conflict on your own and in shorter order than you might think. You have great power to resolve an interpersonal conflict if you know where to focus your effort.

- **Freedom can be more important than joint resolution**. Not all conflict requires you to find a resolution with the other person in order to find your peace of mind.

Conflict Hooks

Real or perceived insults to your identity and unresolved identity needs are at the heart of many recurring conflict problems. A "conflict hook" is a part of your identity that has become snagged by the insult, causing conflict or escalating it. The conflict pivot practices help you discern and manage your conflict hooks, which typically fall in one or more of the following six broad categories:

1. **Competence:** the need to be recognized as capable, intelligent, skilled, or having expertise
2. **Autonomy:** the need to be acknowledged as independent and self-reliant, and having our boundaries respected
3. **Fellowship:** the need to be included and to be viewed as likable, cooperative, and worthy
4. **Status:** the need to be admired for tangible and intangible assets such as reputation, power, attractiveness, and material worth
5. **Reliability:** the need to be seen as trustworthy,

dependable, and loyal

6. **Integrity:** the need for others to respect our dignity, honor, virtue, and good character

You may be snagged by any of these conflict hooks, though it is likely that you have one or two hooks that are most pronounced and tend to snag you more frequently than others. Your conflict hooks are your own, sourced from your family, work, faith, and educational roots. People around you may have some of the same pronounced conflict hooks that you do, or very different ones. Two people snagged by the same conflict may have very different conflict hooks that snagged them.

The Three Pivots

Pivot 1: Away from your stuck story and toward its message

Like a movie trailer, your stuck story of the conflict is a montage of the moments you find most compelling, with certain scenes magnified and others omitted. It's the story you may tell others about the conflict, and the one you tell yourself, often over and over. But it's not *the* story of the conflict; it's *your* story of the conflict. The first pivot is to turn your attention away from your stuck story and toward the message it's holding for you. You accomplish this by:

- identifying what you've reacted to most strongly in the conflict; and
- noticing what you dwell on most when you tell

your stuck story to yourself and others.

Pivot 2: Away from their behavior and toward your conflict hooks

Conflict occurs when something important feels threatened. The things you're dwelling on and reacting to most are hints about the true source of your uneasiness; that source is often your very identity. The second pivot is to turn your attention away from the things the other person is doing (or not doing) and toward the underlying reasons you are hooked. You accomplish this by:

- using what you dwell on and react to most strongly to help you identify the true source of your discomfort; and
- identifying your conflict hooks.

Pivot 3: Away from the past and toward the now

Conflict thrives in the unknowable past and in your reliance on the other person(s) to set things right. Conflict resolution is an act of the present and future. The third pivot is to turn your attention away from what's happened and toward what's next. You accomplish this by:

- figuring out what you want for yourself from here forward, including how to best address your identity needs; and
- identifying solutions that do not require the other person's contribution for you to achieve them.

When to Pivot

You can pivot at any stage in a conflict. While pivots are most easily achieved outside the "heat of the moment," when you have time to reflect, with familiarity they can also help you change your reactions in the midst of high-heat encounters.

Pivoting very early in a conflict, perhaps when you first notice tension or a small flare of anger, will help you avoid getting deeply hooked by the conflict and help you change the way the conflict unfolds. Indeed, pivoting early may help you avoid a conflict altogether.

If you are facing a conflict that was already difficult by the time you learned about conflict pivots, pivoting will help you view the conflict in new ways and figure out how to free yourself from it for the long run.

RESOURCES

Hungry for more about conflict pivots, conflict hooks, and turning conflict into peace of mind? Visit the book's website:

lenski.com/conflictpivot

...and find resources like these:

- a downloadable copy of *The Conflict Pivot Worksheet*;
- printable one-page guide to the three pivots, suitable for posting on your bulletin board and sharing with friends, family, and colleagues;
- book club materials, including discussion guide and questions to ponder together;
- interviews with Tammy, added as they're available;
- success stories from readers, added as they become available;
- answers to questions from readers like you, along with a form to submit your own questions;
- Tammy's blog, *Conflict Zen*, with weekly fresh ideas about conflict resolution and conflict pivots and access to the blog's archives with hundreds of past conflict resolution and negotiation articles.

NOTES

Introduction

1. Client names and identifying details have been heavily disguised throughout the book to protect confidentiality. The names of others, including my graduate students, have generally not been changed unless requested.

2. I've been testing the ideas in this book on my blog and in speeches for years. The blog posts and speeches number in the hundreds. I've elected not to cite each of them because the sheer volume is prohibitive. Since I am aware of the academic concept of "self-plagiarism," this note is to acknowledge use of my own ideas.

Chapter 1

1. Portia Nelson, *There's a Hole in My Sidewalk: The Romance of Self-Discovery* (Hillsboro, OR: Beyond Words Publishing, 1993), 2–3.

2. Adapted from a koan in Paul Reps, *Zen Flesh, Zen Bones: A Collection of Zen and Pre-Zen Writings* (Rutland, VT: Tuttle Publishing, 1957), 33–34.

3. Derek Sivers, August 7, 2004, "Say NO by Default," *O'Reilly ONLamp Blog*, http://www.oreillynet.com/onlamp/blog/2004/08/say_no_by_default.html.

4. As quoted in 37signals, *Getting Real: The Smarter, Faster, Easier Way to Build a Successful Web Application* (Chicago, IL: 37signals, 2006), 39.

5. Mark Milian, October 6, 2011, "The Spiritual Side of Steve Jobs," *CNN Tech*, http://www.cnn.com/2011/10/05/tech/innovation/steve-jobs-philosophy/index.html.

6. Craig Runde, "Conflict and Your Career: An Effectiveness Study," *ACResolution*, Winter 2003: 8.

7. Eric Ries, June 22, 2009, "Pivot, Don't Jump to a New Vision," *Startup Lessons Learned Blog*, http://www.startuplessonslearned.com/2009/06/pivot-dont-jump-to-new-vision.html.

8. Reps, *Zen Flesh, Zen Bones: A Collection of Zen and Pre-Zen Writings*, 19.

9. Thomas Moore, *Dark Nights of the Soul: A Guide to Finding Your Way through Life's Ordeals* (New York: Gotham, 1994), Kindle Edition, chap. 1.

Chapter 2

1. James W. Pennebaker, "Writing about Emotional Experiences as a Therapeutic Process," *Psychological Science*, 8 (1997): 162–66.

Chapter 3

1. "The Magic of Myth: Storytelling and the Psyche," narrated by Natasha Mitchell, All in the Mind, September 7, 2003, http://www.abc.net.au/radionational/programs/allinthe mind/the-magic-of-myth-storytelling-and-the-psyche/3545550.

2. Paul Elie, *The Life You Save Might Be Your Own: An American Pilgrimage* (New York: Farrar, Straus, and Giroux, 2003).

3. Joan Didion, *The White Album* (New York: Simon and Schuster, 1979).

4. Lynn Hasher, David Goldstein, and Thomas Toppino, "Frequency and the Conference of Referential Validity," *Journal of Verbal Learning and Verbal Behavior*, 16 (1977): 107–12.

5. Ian Maynard Begg, Ann Anas, and Suzanne Farinacci, "Dissociation of Processes in Belief: Source Recollection, Statement Familiarity, and the Illusion of Truth. *Journal of Experimental Psychology: General*, 121(1992): 446–58.

6. Jason D. Ozubko and Jonathan Fugelsang, "Remembering Makes Evidence Compelling: Retrieval from Memory Can Give Rise to the Illusion of Truth," *Journal of Experimental Psychology: Learning, Memory, and Cognition*, 37 (2011): 270–76.

7. Melanie C. Green and Timothy C. Brock, "The Role of Transportation in the Persuasiveness of Public Narratives," *Journal of Personality and Social Psychology*, 79 (2000): 701–21.

8. Christopher Chabris and Daniel Simons, The Invisible Gorilla and Other Ways Our Intuition Deceives Us (New York: HarperCollins, 2010), Kindle Edition, chap. 2.

9. Jeremy Dean, October 2010, "How Memory Works: 10 Things Most People Get Wrong," *PsyBlog*, http://www.spring.org.uk/2012/10/how-memory-works-10-things-most-people-get-wrong.php.

10. Daniel H. Weiss, August 8, 2011, "We Do Not See Things as They Are, We See Things as We Are," *Humanities and Social Sciences Online*, http://h-net.msu.edu/cgi-bin/logbrowse.pl?trx=vx&list=H-Judaic&month=1108&msg=RizwZWCgeA8woVU9mNOEYQ.

11. Dalai Lama, n.d., "A Human Approach to World Peace," *His Holiness the 14th Dalai Lama of Tibet*, http://www.dalailama.com/messages/world-peace/a-human-approach-to-peace.

12. Moore, *Dark Nights of the Soul: A Guide to Finding Your Way through Life's Ordeals*, chap. 10.

13. Thomas Moore, *Original Soul: Living with Paradox and Originality* (New York: HarperColllins, 2000).

14. John Winslade and Gerald D. Monk, *Narrative Mediation: A New Approach to Conflict Resolution* (San Francisco, CA: Jossey-Bass, 2000).

15. Brad J. Bushman, Angelica M. Bonacci, William C. Pedersen, Eduardo A. Vasquez, and Norman Miller, "Chewing on It Can Chew You Up: Effects of Rumination on Triggered Displaced Aggression," *Journal of Personality and Social Psychology*, 88 (2005): 969–83.

16. Dominik Mischkowski, Ethan Kross, and Brad J. Bushman, "Flies on the Wall Are Less Aggressive: Self-Distancing in the Heat of the Moment Reduces Aggressive Thoughts, Angry Feelings, and Aggressive Behavior," *Journal of Experimental Social Psychology* (2012): doi:10.1016/j.jesp.2012.03.012.

17. Stephen M. Shick, *Consider the Lilies: Meditations* (Boston, MA: Skinner House Books, 2004), 37.

Chapter 4

1. Donald G. Dutton and Arthur P. Aron, "Some Evidence for Heightened Sexual Attraction under Conditions of High Anxiety," *Journal of Personality and Social Psychology*, 30 (1974): 510–17.

2. Carl G. Jung, *Memories, Dreams, Reflections* (New York: Pantheon Books, 1963).

3. Jeffrey Kottler, *Beyond Blame: A New Way of Resolving Conflicts in Relationships* (San Francisco, CA: Jossey-Bass, 1994), 59–76.

4. Mark Epstein, July 1, 1995, "Opening Up to Happiness," *Psychology Today Blog*, http://www.psychologytoday.com/articles/200910/opening-happiness.

5. Don Miguel Ruiz, *The Four Agreements: A Practical Guide to Personal Freedom* (San Rafael, CA: Amber-Allen Publishing, 1997).

6. Thích Nhất Hạnh, *Anger: Wisdom for Cooling the Flames* (New York: Penguin, 2001), 29.

7. Tsoknyi Rinpoche, April 3, 2012, "Real but Not True," *Huffington Post Blog*, http://www.huffingtonpost.com/Tsoknyi-rinpoche/emotions_b_1398325.html.

8. Moore, *Dark Nights of the Soul: A Guide to Finding Your Way through Life's Ordeals*, chap. 1.

9. Douglas Stone, Bruce Patton, and Sheila Heen, *Difficult Conversations: How to Discuss What Matters Most* (New York: Viking, 1999), 113.

10. Stella Ting-Toomey, "The Matrix of Face: An Updated Face-Negotiation Theory," in *Theorizing about Intercultural Communication*, ed. William B. Gudykunst (Thousand Oaks, CA: Sage Publications, 2005), 71–92.

11. Kottler, *Beyond Blame: A New Way of Resolving Conflicts in Relationships*, 30.

12. I was given a copy of this story years ago on a blank piece of paper and have never been able to track down the original source. If you know it, please share so that I can give credit where credit is due.

13. Peter M. Senge, *The Fifth Discipline: The Art and Practice of the Learning Organization.* (New York: Doubleday/Currency, 1990), 57.

Chapter 5

1. Jimmy Carter, *Keeping Faith: Memoirs of a President* (New York: Bantam, 1982), 408.

2. William Jefferson Clinton, "Foreword," In *Mandela: The Authorized Portrait*, eds. Mac Maharaj and Ahmad Kathrada (Kansas City, MO: Andrews McMeel Publishing, 2006).

3. Mark Nepo, *The Book of Awakening: Having the Life You Want by Being Present to the Life You Have* (Berkeley, CA: Conari Press, 2000).

4. Kottler, *Beyond Blame: A New Way of Resolving Conflicts in Relationships*, 76.

Chapter 6

1. Christopher Alexander, *The Timeless Way of Building* (New York: Oxford University Press, 1979).

2. Allan Lokos, *Pocket Peace: Effective Practices for Enlightened Living* (New York: Tarcher, 2010), Kindle Edition, chap. 10.

3. Allison S. Troy, Amanda J. Shallcross, and Iris B. Mauss, "A Person-By-Situation Approach to Emotion Regulation: Cognitive Reappraisal Can Either Help or Hurt, Depending on the Context," *Psychological Science*, 24 (2013): 2505–14.

4. Peter Senge, Art Kleiner, Charlotte Roberts, Richard Ross, and Bryan Smith, *The Fifth Discipline Fieldbook: Strategies and Tools for Building a Learning Organization* (New York: Currency, Doubleday, 1994), 242–6.

5. Christopher C. Berger and H. Henrik Ehrsson, "Mental Imagery Changes Multisensory Perception. *Current Biology*, 23 (2013): 1367–72.

6. Jay Rothman, *Resolving Identity-Based Conflict in Nations, Organizations, and Communities* (San Francisco, CA: Jossey-Bass, 1997).

7. *I Am*, directed by Tom Shadyac (Universal City, CA: Shady Acres Film, 2010), DVD.

Chapter 7

1. Benjamin Franklin, John Bigelow, and Bruce Rogers, *The Autobiography of Benjamin Franklin* (New York: Houghton Mifflin & Company, 1906), 91.

2. Sam Kaner, *Facilitator's Guide to Participatory Decision-Making* (San Francisco, CA: John Wiley & Sons, 2007), 19.

3. Candy Chang's Facebook page, accessed March 20, 2014, https://www.facebook.com/BeforeIDieWall.

Made in the USA
Lexington, KY
11 November 2014